SAVED BUT STRUGGLING, WELL BUT WOUNDED

THE BENEFITS OF PROFESSIONAL CHRISTIAN COUNSELING

ERIC JOSEPH

Book paperback edition: October 2024

Book design, Cover design, and eBook design by: Word-2-Kindle Publisher: Amazon KDP

Hardback ISBN | 979-8-9877156-2-8

Library of Congress Control Number: 2023905155

www.totaltherapytoday.com

Foreword

Eric Joseph is a great friend and companion in the gospel of Jesus Christ, a man with a passion for helping others to recover from all their shortcomings and helping to identify potential in people from all walks of life. His experience as a pastor, teacher, and counselor guides him into the hearts of humanity to help them capture the greater essence of life and living.

Eric's book aims to unravel the myth of pretense contentedness during crises and points to the benefits of professional Christian counseling. Eric uncovers the Biblical truth in counseling. He also points to a greater dimension in the quest to achieve holistic wellness through professional counseling that will meet the needs of struggling Christians who are spiritually motivated yet lack emotional and psychological stability.

Eric is a thoughtful counselor who sees the need for professional counseling among Christians. He is a counselor and pastor who seeks to empower people with the necessary tools and information to assist them in their quest towards a healthy, spiritual, emotional, and temporal lifestyle of stability. His passion for counseling makes him desire to reach a wide cross-section of society, offering his experience and wisdom to readers, motivating Christians and non-Christians alike to take advantage of the opportunity available to them, which will no doubt play a pivotal role in the upliftment of lives.

Eric highlights the urgent need for a closer look at Christian counseling and sees this as his responsibility to help prepare men and women for this new awakening in the Christian community. His work emphasizes various areas relevant to human development and advancement through professional Christian counseling. Eric presents twenty-six areas of vital information relevant and effective to counseling that will serve as an informative tool for successful living.

Eric addresses a whole gamut of human psychology, stressing the need for intervention, avoiding stigmas, and seeking help. He calls upon his readers to ignore negative vibes and seek professional Christian counseling to help secure a more stable family, relationships, and spiritual connection with the divine. He believes in spiritual counseling and encourages his readers to capitalize on professional counseling, not to spiritualize everything, but to allow the opportunity to look deeply into human thinking with open minds to garner more information that will bring sustainability.

Eric invites readers to glean into this book and discover the valuable asset he presents, which will pave the way for a healthy and holistic life. Therefore, I highly recommend this masterpiece of professional undertaking to all readers.

Aubrey C. H. Brown Jr. Th. D., Ph. D Candidate at Newburgh Theological Seminary.

Dedication

This book is lovingly dedicated to my amazing wife Amy, saying thanks for being an ongoing tower of inspiration, support, and strength. You have contributed to this book in many ways including editing and organizing its content. Thanks for helping me stay focused on completing this book which started many years ago. I am also thankful for my two awesome princesses Jem and Tiffany, who bring joy to my heart daily. You made fun of all my suggested cover page pictures but your input made a difference in the final product. Love and blessings to my beautiful family!

I also want to say a special thanks to Cheo Ramlochan, who was instrumental in helping to develop the image on the inside of this book. I will also give a big thank you to all those who have sacrificed their time to ensure that this book was well-written and relatable. These individuals include Cherryann McLeod, Drexel Perry Jr., Mr. Josh Hector, Licensed Therapist, Pastor Dan Whitney, and Andria Smith. I cannot complete this dedication page without acknowledging the encouragement and prayer support from my Church Avenue Church of God family.

CONTENTS

PROLOGUE

Here are 15 sobering statistics about the state of mental health in the U.S.A.

- One in five Americans suffers from a mental illness (NIMH) (nimh.nih.gov).

- Anxiety disorders are the highest reported mental health issue in the US with 42.5 million Americans claiming to suffer from this illness. (Mental Health America) (mhanational.org).

- Mental illnesses start showing symptoms by age 14 (National Alliance on Mental Illness) (nami.org),

- About one in four American adults suffers from a diagnosable mental disorder in a given year, and one in 10 will suffer from a depressive illness, such as major depression or bipolar disorder (Johns Hopkins) (hopkinismedicine.org).

- Mental health crises account for 60 million visits to primary care and six million ER visits annually. (Centers for Disease Control and Prevention) (cdc.gov).

- 41 percent of Americans dealt with an untreated mental illness. (Mental Health First Aid) (mentalhealthfirst aid.org).

- 40 million Americans suffer from anxiety (Anxiety and Depression Association of America). Almost six in 10

1

people with mental illness get no treatment or medication (adaa.org/thezebra.com.

- In 2019, an estimated 47.6 million adults (19% of the country) had a mental illness, but only 43% received any kind of mental health care (thezebra.com).
- More than 40,000 Americans die annually from suicide (usatoday.com).
- Mental health illness rates were significantly higher for adolescents (about 50%) and young adults (about 30%) (ahmc.com).
- Women experience depression at roughly twice the rate of men (mayoclinic.org).
- An estimated 26% of Americans aged 18 and older suffer from a diagnosable mental disorder (hopkinsmedicine.org).
- Almost half of Americans will experience an episode of mental illness in their lives (mentalhealthfirstaid.org).
- There are 4.5 million children in the United States diagnosed and living with anxiety (thezebra.com).
- ADHD, behavior problems, anxiety, and depression are the most common mental disorders affecting children (cdc.gov).

I do not believe that it is the plan of God for his children to needlessly suffer when there is help available. God's word declares that He would supply all our needs (Philippians 4:19 KJV). Professional Christian counseling is one of God's blessings available to the body of Christ. It's a gift and ministry, so let's gladly embrace and use it. Professional Christian counseling is an answer to prayers. It is another method or avenue God frequently uses so His children can experience total healing today!

CHAPTER 1
Is that in the bible?

Today, there are many Christians who see professional counseling as unbiblical, unnecessary, or unhelpful. However, the Bible often affirms the importance and value of seeking counsel when making plans or desiring wisdom for direction and general decision-making. For the Christian, it is imperative to consult the Lord and a competent counselor-servant/minister who can help one achieve a desired goal. This book is purposely designed to explore and address the Biblical and psychological reasons why it is beneficial for Christians/believers to seek professional counseling.

Many scriptures lend such credence. To begin with, the book of Isaiah 9:6 says, "For unto us a child is born, unto us a son is given: and the government shall be upon his shoulder: and his name shall be called Wonderful, Counsellor, The mighty God, The everlasting Father, The Prince of Peace." (KJV). Embedded in this verse is the word Counselor which is one of God's divine attributes. I wish to share another scripture on the word counsel before I address its definitions and concepts. Isaiah 11:2 says, "And the spirit of the LORD shall rest upon him, the spirit of wisdom and understanding, the spirit of counsel and might, the spirit of knowledge and the fear of the LORD;" (KJV). Here again, we see the spirit of counsel manifested in Jesus, the son of God. The Hebrew word for 'counseling' is 'etsah,' which means advice. In Strong's Concordance, the term is 'yaats,' which also means to advise. In Strong's Exhaustive Concordance, the primitive root of the word means to deliberate, resolve, or guide.

The word 'counseling' can have multiple meanings, including offering advice and encouragement, sharing wisdom and skills, setting goals, resolving conflict, etc. Counselors usually probe the past to repair the present, whether the problem happened a week ago or during childhood. Sometimes they collaborate with medical practitioners to explore possible side effects of physical and chemical imbalances that can cause psychological problems. A significant part of counseling is addressing issues, resolving conflicts, and restoring relationships between people. Much will be said about counseling throughout this book.

A good scenario of this practice is seen in Exodus 18:13–22 (NLT), which can be described as Jethro's wise counsel. [13] "The next day, Moses took his seat to hear the people's disputes against each other. They waited before him from morning till evening. [14] When Moses' father-in-law saw all that Moses was doing for the people, he asked, 'What are you really accomplishing here? Why are you trying to do all this alone while everyone stands around you from morning till evening?' [15] Moses replied, 'Because the people come to me to get a ruling from God. [16] When a dispute arises, they come to me, and I am the one who settles the case between the quarreling parties. I inform the people of God's decrees and give them his instructions.' ¹⁷ 'This is not good!' Moses' father-in-law exclaimed. ¹⁸ 'You're going to wear yourself out—and the people, too. This job is too heavy a burden for you to handle all by yourself. ¹⁹ Now listen to me, and let me give you a word of advice, and may God be with you. You should continue to be the people's representative before God, bringing their disputes to him. ²⁰ Teach them God's decrees, and give them his instructions. Show them how to conduct their lives. ²¹ But select from all the people some capable, honest men who fear God and hate bribes. Appoint them as leaders over groups of one thousand, one hundred, fifty, and ten. ²² They should always be available to solve the people's common disputes but have them bring the major cases to you. Let the leaders decide the smaller matters themselves. They will help you carry the load, making the task easier for you.'"

We can further note in the Bible that the Spirit of counsel was upon Jesus who now lives in us and therefore enables us to give effective counsel to others. Proverbs 12:15 says, ¹⁵ "The way of a fool *is* right in his own eyes, but he who heeds counsel *is* wise."

According to the "law of first mention," the first time the root word for counsel appears in the Bible would strongly indicate its expected use. While Moses meant well and wanted the best for his people, the job was 'too heavy' for him, so he needed help. If Moses did not get help, he would eventually succumb to the mental, emotional, and physical weight of the workload. Can you imagine the consistent weight of this responsibility upon this man of God?

Jethro, Moses' father-in-law gave him some good advice which was sure to reduce the stress in his life. From all indications, he had Moses' best interest at heart. He spoke the truth in love as the Apostle Paul said in Ephesians 4:15, which said, [5] Instead, we will speak the truth in love, growing in every way more and more like Christ, who is the head of his body, the church. Jethro's advice was well received, as we can see in Exodus 18:24(NLT), "Moses listened to his father-in-law's advice and followed his suggestions." Such an approach to addressing the vicissitudes of life is still warranted and available to us today.

Proverbs 11:14 (KJV) says, "Where no counsel is, the people fall: but in the multitude of counselors there is safety." Proverbs 15:22 (KJV) says, "Without counsel purposes are disappointed: but in the multitude of counselors they are established."

"The heartfelt counsel of a friend is as sweet as perfume and incense." Proverbs 27:9 (NLT). James 1:5 says, "If you need wisdom, ask a generous God, and he will give it to you. He will not rebuke you for asking."

Based on what you may be experiencing at this time in your life, what kind of counseling do you think might benefit you?

CHAPTER 2
What is Counseling?

The Merriam-Webster Learner's Dictionary defines counseling as advice and support given to people to help them deal with problems, make important decisions, etc. Merriam-Webster dictionary defines the word counsel as advice given, especially as a result of consultation. The emphasis in this book relates to professional Christian counseling.

Hence, the question, what is professional Christian counseling? Professional Christian counseling integrates Christianity and Psychology in a Christ-centered, Bible-based, and Holy Spirit-led way, bringing wholeness to one's life. Christian counselors believe that God is the author of all truths. Christian counselors evaluate and consider the mental, emotional, relational, and spiritual needs of others and use prayer and the Bible to provide strength, direction, wisdom, and healing, that goes beyond man-made techniques and interventions.

To understand the relevance and importance of professional Christian counseling, we must understand the tripartite nature of man. Professional Christian counseling aims to help Christians achieve personal wholeness, interpersonal competence, mental and emotional stability, and spiritual maturity. The Bible's defense for this threefold approach is expressed in the book of Genesis 2:7 (KJV), which states, "The LORD God formed man from the dust of the ground, and breathed into his nostrils the breath of life; and man became a living soul."

Hebrews 4:12 (KJV) states, 12 "For the word of God is quick, and powerful, and sharper than any two-edged sword, piercing even to the dividing asunder of soul and spirit, and of the joints and marrow, and is a discerner of the thoughts and intents of the heart." We also read in 1 Thessalonians 5:23 (NLT), "Now may the God of peace make you holy in every way, and may your whole spirit and soul and body be kept blameless until our Lord Jesus Christ comes again."

The word 'soul' appears in all three scriptures. So, we can conclude that man comprises three components: body, soul, and spirit. The body is a person's physical structure or material part, including the bones, flesh, and organs. It is the body that houses or accommodates man's spirit and soul. The body, sometimes called the flesh, is the medium that manifests the works of the spirit or the soul.

Now let's take a look at the definition of the soul. The soul is the immaterial part of man, composed of the mind, will, and emotions. It cannot be physically touched or seen. The five senses of smell, taste, touch, hearing, and sight are operated in the soulish realm. We can also describe the soul as the seat of self-consciousness. It is important also to mention here that man is not only tripartite but also a triune being. This means

9

that his body, soul, and spirit are all interconnected and interrelated.

The spirit is the immaterial intelligent part of a person. This is where elements of praise and worship to God occur when the human spirit is regenerated or born again. John 4:24 (NLT) says, "God is a Spirit: and they that worship him must worship him in spirit and in truth."

Here is a diagram that expresses both the tripartite and the triune nature of man:

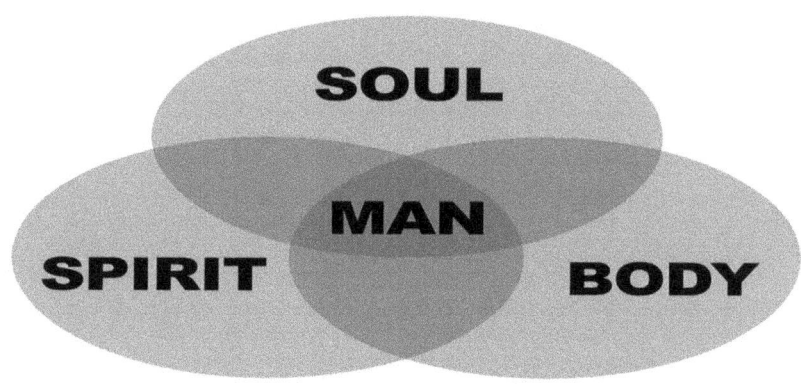

This means that whatever impacts or affects a man's physical body also impacts his soul and spirit. Whatever affects his soul also impacts his spirit and body, and whatever affects his spirit also impacts his body and soul.

We can see one example of this in the term 'psychosomatic.' The Greek word for 'soul' is 'psyche' and the Greek word for 'body ' is 'soma.'It means relating to, involving, or concerned with bodily symptoms caused by mental or emotional disturbance. So, psychosomatic is a physical illness or other condition caused or aggravated by a mental factor such as internal conflict or stress or a physical illness or condition relating to the interaction of mind and body.

One of the things that would also happen when someone has a psychosomatic situation is that they also tend to draw from a belief system that can help them through that situation. In other words, the situation has also impacted the person's spirit.

CHAPTER 3
Why Seek Help

This book is about making a case for professional Christian counseling, and why it is beneficial and should be seen as normal to seek help when experiencing personal, emotional, relational, and spiritual difficulties. When a Christian becomes sick, more often than not, their first response is to seek help from a physician. On the other hand, when that person needs a miracle or spiritual help, they will pray to the Lord or speak with their pastor. So far, we can generally agree that talking with God and the clergy is the approach in which our spiritual needs are met, and the physician takes care of our bodily or physical needs.

Remember that the soul is made up of the mind, will, and emotions. The mind is where our thought processing takes place. This is where we exercise our mental abilities to think rightly or wrongly, positively or negatively. The will is where the power to make decisions rests, whether they are right or wrong. In the soulish realm, emotions or feelings, be they positive or negative, are manufactured and expressed. Based on this analysis, we can conclude that it is in the soulish realm that we get to know one another and can relate to one another.

Now, when we experience personal and relationship difficulties in various situations and are hurt or wounded in the process, where do we go to seek help? Can you see the missing link? Spirit... God, Body... Physician, Soul...? **We can go to God for spiritual help, and we can go to the doctor for physical or bodily help, but who do we go to for soulish, emotional, and mental help?**

Quite often, because counseling is perceived as taboo, an emotionally wounded or mentally troubled person would seek medical help, unlike mental and emotional help. The truth is that God is the ultimate healer and, more often than not, frequently uses his servants/ministers, physicians, and professional counselors to help facilitate the process of change, growth, and health for all of us.

From this explanation, we can say that God ministers to the spirit, the physician ministers to the body, and the professional counselor ministers to the soul, which comprises the mind, emotions, and will.

There are some core issues in professional Christian counseling that must be recognized. To those who may have never sought professional Christian counseling, this information would help put you at ease.

Professional Christian counseling is not just telling someone about your 'business' – who may tell someone else. It is not paying someone to tell you what or what not to do. It is not about you feeling belittled or embarrassed. Instead, this unique type of counseling addresses core aspects of your life that can help you live out your fullest potential.

These core components are:

- Exploring personal issues, purpose, and desire.

- Establishing meaningful relationships with Jesus Christ and with others.

- Developing Biblical self-worth, cognition, decision-making, and behaviors and pursuing a wholesome state of being.

"Professional Christian counseling is about helping you move to personal wholeness, interpersonal competence, mental and emotional stability, and spiritual maturity." Who would not want to achieve such remarkable results? I also strongly believe that this is God's plan for each of our lives, and we should not settle for less.

Resistance to seeking help

This might be a good place to talk about resistance to seeking professional counseling. Even though the information that I am sharing here is about males in general, there is not much difference between a non-Christian male and a Christian male except that one is a Christian and the other is not. However, the reality is that the issues of this life do impact both Christians and non-Christians.

According to Skovolt (1978), men find it difficult to express feelings openly, give up emotional control, and be vulnerable to themselves, others, and new experiences. That is called 'restrictive emotionality.' Balswick (1982) described the male as one who does not verbally express his feelings or was socialized not to do so. He called that 'male inexpressiveness.'

From those two statements, it seems that the situation remains the same even in the 21st century. On the other hand, women, who are generally more emotional than men, tend to be the ones who would initiate counseling. I applaud the women and hope that Christian males understand that part of God-given leadership includes preserving the relational and emotional stability of their lives, marriages, and family.

Among the ethnic groups, it seems that African Americans are more resistant to counseling. Let's look at a few reasons for their reluctance. Firstly, the psycho-historic impact of slavery and the Tuskegee experience caused an African American distrust of governmental entities. The negative impact of those historic occurrences should instead give African Americans reasons to seek counseling to explore those unresolved issues. Another reason for African Americans' resistance to seeking professional counseling would be the issue of discrimination. This feeling of inferiority and subservience which may also be a byproduct of slavery, would have to be addressed since it can hinder one from experiencing emotional freedom.

The psychological and emotional wounds of slavery have indeed created a deficit of trust within the African American community, and again such issues have to be worked on because they will not just go away by magic. Because African Americans are a collectivistic society, privacy is a priority that they guard aggressively. Could it be that African Americans and, more so, Caribbean Americans have not appropriately conceptualized what counseling is? Part of this issue is that the idea of professional counseling has never been a part of their cultural narrative.

Instead, we have learned that 'what happens at home stays at home,' which is not the truth. **The reality in most cases** is that when the situation becomes overbearing, they tend to seek advice beyond families and friends from peers and the elderly, which in many cases may not be very fruitful since those 'advisors' would have developed unhealthy coping skills which they continue to pass down, hence becoming a perpetuated generational practice.

There needs to be a cognitive shift within the African American and Caribbean-American communities since this traditional approach has had little or no success, as recognized by the present state of marriages and families. If we keep doing what we have always done, we will continue to experience the disintegration of the Black family. As Christians, however, we have a Biblical obligation to fight for our families in every area of their lives, which includes emotional and psychological stability.

Another reason why many Christians may be resistant to professional counseling is because of the fear of being diagnosed with a mental health disorder. This is a legitimate fear, and there is a stigma to it, especially within the African American community. Mental health diseases are just like any other diseases or sicknesses as hypertension, high cholesterol, cancer, diabetes, and asthma. They all are a result of the consequences of Adamic sin and bad decision-making.

Before you accuse me of theological malpractice, I believe,

based upon the word of God, that being a Christian does not exempt us from the vicious impact of sin. While our spirit has been regenerated, until Christ comes or until we die, we will still experience various struggles within our souls and bodies. Even creation is experiencing the impact of sin.

Romans 8:19–22 (NLT) says, [19] "For all creation is waiting eagerly for that future day when God will reveal who his children are. [20] Against its will, all creation was subjected to God's curse. But with eager hope, [21] the creation looks forward to the day when it will join God's children in glorious freedom from death and decay. [22] For we know that all creation has been groaning as in the pains of childbirth right up to the present time."

Galatians 5:17–20 says, [17] "For the desires of the flesh are against the Spirit, and the desires of the Spirit are against the flesh, for these are opposed to each other, to keep you from doing the things you want to do. [18] But if you are led by the Spirit, you are not under the law. [19] Now the works of the flesh are evident: sexual immorality, impurity, sensuality, [20] idolatry, sorcery, enmity, strife, jealousy, fits of anger, rivalries, dissensions, divisions [21] and envy; drunkenness, orgies, and the like. I warn you, as I did before, that those who live like this will not inherit the kingdom of God."

What happens in our body, or how we behave, is determined by who controls the messages received by either the Soul or the spirit. We sin when we allow the soul to control the message.

On the contrary, when we give heed to the spirit, the result is stated in verses 22–24, which states, [22] "But the fruit of the Spirit is love, joy, peace, patience, kindness, goodness, faithfulness,

[23] gentleness and self-control. Against such things, there is no law. [24] Those who belong to Christ Jesus have crucified the sinful nature with its passions and desires."

CHAPTER 4
Whom Should I Talk To?

Concerning the topic of Christianity and mental illness, a common question that many may ask is, should a Christian seek help from a psychologist or psychiatrist?

According to Jay Adams, author, and founder of the modern Biblical counseling movement related that many Christians struggle with the decision to see a psychologist or psychiatrist as the key to overcoming mental illness. Christian psychologists, psychiatrists, and counselors are numerous, and Christians seek their advice regularly, most often for depression and anxiety. Part of the difficulty is that there is a wide variety of psychological disorders, some emotional and some physical, but all have a spiritual component.[4]

A source of depression or anxiety can stem from leading a sinful lifestyle. For a genuine follower of Christ, it's crucial to recognize that God awaits our confession and repentance, offering spiritual, mental, and emotional healing in return.

For a Christian, the influence and oppression of demons can extend to the point of causing mental illness. It's essential to bear in mind that Christians cannot be possessed by evil spirits or influenced beyond manageable temptation (1 Corinthians 10:13). This is because believers are already indwelled with the

The Spirit of God (Romans 8:9–11), and the Holy Spirit do not coexist with demons in the same 'residence.'

Another thing people often do not consider is that God has allowed mankind to invent and develop many different kinds of medicines for healing. Medication may be necessary if a person has a true mental illness caused by hormonal or chemical imbalances in the brain. It is no different from going to a doctor to get medicine for an injury or physical illness. Similarly, God has blessed some Christian counselors and psychologists with supernatural insight, and the ability to accurately evaluate a person and get to the true root of the problem. To ignore such giftedness seems unwise.

Whether or not to seek help from a Christian psychologist is a personal decision. It is a matter of conscience because the Bible does not specifically address the issue. Here are some things to consider that may help determine the need to seek professional Christian counseling.

1. Does my behavior affect others, especially my family? Has my behavior negatively impacted my peer relationships, school, or job performance?

2. Is my illness causing me to disobey God and refuse to allow the Holy Spirit to work through me?

3. Is my witness for Christ suffering because of this disability?

If you know you are sick, but refuse to get help for selfish reasons, that is sinful. If it is strongly against your belief system to seek psychiatric care, and you have spent time in prayer and meditation, you should discuss any alternatives with your doctor and pastor or minister.

It is not sinful to see a psychiatrist, psychologist, or counselor. Doing so does not show a lack of faith in God, although we should always go to God first for healing and direction. He wants to be in charge of every part of our lives, and we should feel free to take our problems to Him in prayer for every situation and every circumstance. God often uses Christian psychologists, therapists, and counselors to bring healing to His children. Seeing a professional Christian counselor or psychiatrist, however, is definitely preferable to a secular therapist who will give advice from a worldly or humanistic point of view instead of a Biblical perspective.

CHAPTER 5
Types of Counseling

As I speak to many Christian concerning the issue of seeking professional counseling, their reactions are mostly negative, as it seems that the word counseling releases a 'bad taste.' Many Christians would comment and believe that whatever they are going through can be fixed on its own. Others think that the situation would go away with time, Bible reading, fasting, and prayer. Unfortunately, in many of those cases, the situation worsens and ultimately negatively impacts everything else around them.

Some problems based upon their nature can be resolved without having an unbearable impact on one's functioning. On the other hand, professional Christian counseling can be of tremendous benefit to those who are willing to face their fears and unwilling to surrender to negative or unhealthy experiences.

Let's look at various types of counseling that you and your loved ones may have used in the past.

School and career counselors

We consider school counselors (once called guidance counselors) and career counselors together. Both counseling specialties deal with people who are seeking career, vocational, and academic advice and guidance. School counselors help evaluate students' abilities, interests, and personalities to develop realistic academic and career goals. It involves assisting students of all levels, from elementary school to college. They use interviews, counseling sessions, and aptitude assessment tests to help determine one's best fit.

Career counselors typically work with people who are in or have finished college. However, some may advise high school students looking to start a career immediately. School and career counselors both advocate for students, or other individuals and organizations, such as a state unemployment office or placement service, to promote academic, career, and social development.

Substance abuse counselors

A substance abuse counselor works directly with clients suffering from substance abuse or dependence. They are called upon to treat people in recovery. They also work to prevent drug and alcohol abuse at an early age by educating parents on how to get involved in their children's exposure to drugs and alcohol.

A substance abuse counselor will work with clients on their addiction to things like alcohol, marijuana, opiates, or any other substance. Substance abuse counselors are also called chemical dependency counselors or addiction counselors. They often work with clients on other addictions like sex and gambling. A substance abuse counselor is used to help guide addicts through their recovery by leading groups, having individual sessions, and intensive case management.

Those counselors will also teach clients about early recovery skills, relapse prevention, the trigger cycle, and ways to live a more positive life while abstaining from drugs and alcohol.

Credit counselors

A credit counselor is a professional who provides financial advice and assistance to individuals who are facing challenges with managing their personal finances, particularly their debts and credit-related issues. These counselors work with consumers to help them understand their financial situation, develop a budget, and create a plan to improve their credit and overall financial health.

Vocational counselors

Vocational counselors explore and assess the client's educational background, training, work history, interests, skills, and personality traits. They may also administer aptitude and achievement tests to assist the client in making informed career decisions. Furthermore, vocational counselors assist individuals in developing their job-search skills and guide clients in finding and applying for jobs. Additionally, they support those facing job loss, job-related stress, or other career transition challenges.

Rehabilitation counselors

Rehabilitation counselors assist individuals in coping with the personal, social, and vocational impacts of disabilities stemming from congenital conditions, illness, accidents, or other causes. They evaluate an individual's strengths and limitations, offer personal and vocational counseling, provide case management support, and coordinate medical care, vocational training, and job placement. Rehabilitation counselors conduct interviews with individuals with disabilities and their families, review educational and medical reports, and collaborate with healthcare professionals, psychologists, employers, and physical, occupational, and speech therapists to ascertain an individual's capabilities and skills. Their primary goal is to enhance an individual's ability to live independently, which involves facilitating and coordinating services with other providers.

Grief counselors

Grief counseling focuses on helping individuals navigate the emotions, thoughts, and memories associated with losing a loved one. While grief can manifest following various types of loss, grief counseling primarily assists people in adjusting to life after the death of a loved one. It aids individuals in recognizing the typical aspects of the grieving process, coping with the pain associated with loss, receiving support to manage the anxieties linked to post-loss life changes, and developing strategies to seek help and engage in self-care.

Mental health counselors

Mental health counselors collaborate with individuals, families, and groups to address issues relating to mental and emotional disorders. Their training encompasses a range of therapeutic techniques used to tackle issues such as depression, anxiety, addiction, substance abuse, suicidal tendencies, stress, trauma, low self-esteem, and grief, among others. Mental health counselors also assist with job and career-related concerns, educational decisions, mental and emotional health challenges, and relationship issues. They may also engage in community outreach, advocacy, and mediation. Some mental health counselors specialize in providing services to older people. These professionals often work closely with other mental health specialists, including psychiatrists, psychologists, clinical social workers, psychiatric nurses, and school counselors.

Marriage and family counselors

Marriage and family therapy is the area in which I was educated and trained. Its specialization draws from family systems theory, principles, and techniques to address and treat mental and emotional disorders. Marriage and family counselors focus on modifying individuals' perceptions and behaviors, improving communication and understanding within family units, and helping prevent family and individual crises. Their work may involve individuals, families, couples, and groups. It's important to note that marriage and family therapy differs from traditional therapy by less emphasizing an identified client or internal psychological conflicts.

Professional Christian counseling, for that matter, would include:

- Resolving pressing issues using prayer and the Bible as the foundation and not techniques, theories, or interventions.

- Renew and strengthen relationships.

- Receiving tools, skills, and knowledge to cope with situations as well as options to address life challenges, all taking place in a non-judgmental atmosphere.

CHAPTER 6
The Clergy's Response

Many Christians grew up believing that they should not have to go to counseling. They should only take their problems to Jesus in prayer, read their Bible, fast, and get filled with the Holy Spirit. Some well-meaning Christians, including pastors, do not have the capacity or professional training to meet the specific needs of the congregants. Instead, they spiritualize every problematic situation with words like, "God's strength is perfect, His grace is sufficient," or tell a struggling member to, "Just keep praying, God is able, He will see you through," or "God has a reason for this," etc.

While many Christians, including members of the clergy, are really loving and caring and have the best interest of those they serve, they do not know how to address situations they do not understand. The easiest response is to spiritualize them.

Sometimes, they may challenge Christians to confess their sins so that they can be healed. Even though a believer's problem is impacting his relationship with God, it does not necessarily mean it is a spiritual problem. It can be a soulish/emotional/mental health issue that neither the clergy or the person may be fully aware of. The hurting believers will then continue to live their lives wounded. It may worsen over time as they continue to spiritualize those issues believing that God will eventually, see them through and that God has a reason for what they are experiencing.

More often than not, when someone is in emotional distress, it manifests as physical, bodily symptoms, such as headaches, joint pains, stomach pains, fatigue, memory problems, etc. What happens then is that the person would first consult their primary physician, which is imperative to rule out any medical condition and is a great first step.

Most Christians prefer to see a medical doctor instead of a professional counselor. However, many of those Christians may not be aware that many of their medical providers seek professional counseling to address their own mental health issues including anxiety, depression, and PTSD, according to the Association of America Medical Colleges.

Believing in the doctor and medication is all good. However, God is the ultimate maker of them all. Just as medical providers, professional Christian councilors are also agents of healing. In many cases, medical doctors would often refer a patient for mental health counseling through their insurance based upon their assessment and presenting problems of the person. By the way, how many Christians are really interested in their doctor's religious beliefs, values, or spiritual life? Their desire is to be healed or get well.

In like manner, professional Christian counselors are 'doctors' in their own rights, based upon their education, knowledge, training, skills, and experiences. Their focus or area of specialty is also coupled with their faith and reliance on the power of God and His word through which their work is accomplished.

Medical doctors may prescribe medications for what may be in many cases addressing the "shoot or symptoms" of the problem and the "root or cause" of the problem which can give rise to new physical/emotional problems due to the side effects of those medications. We must indeed trust God in all situations. Still, it is very beneficial for us to identify what is creating the situation.

One common expression or response that I hear from most Christians facing difficulties is "I am praying about it." My response to them would usually be "Praying is great, but what do you do after you have prayed"? Sometimes Christians are reluctant to seek professional help, believing that if only they had more faith, their problems would go away.

The Christian writer and expositor, J. Oswald Sanders, encourages such people to see counseling as another means God can use to bring healing. "One of the things we sometimes do as Christians is narrow the opportunities by which God might help us. One of the ways I think God can bring healing is through counseling. It's not the only way, but counseling represents one more way the Lord can help us."

In his book *The Benefits of Christian Counseling*, John Clark writes, "How has Christian counseling helped me? One, it has helped me identify the causes of my hurts, Two, it has shown me how my childhood has influenced my adult life. Three, I have begun to see how problems have common elements. Fourth, many of my problems are behavior patterns that can be changed. Five, there has been discussion relating to how religious upbringing can cause problems later in life. Six, it has provided emotional support with comfort, but sometimes with the stark reality of what I need to change. Seven, it has helped me to recognize that here is a mind-body connection. These are all areas which may require counseling."[7]

"A good and competent Christian counselor will give advice and answers not just to state authority but to God. That counselor will be one who will pray with and for you not just before and after the sessions, and you will be part of the counselor's prayer list for daily interceding. A counselor who will turn to the Bible for direction instead of just Jung and Freud. One who will not just restore relationships one with another but with God as well."

CHAPTER 7
The Impact of Hidden Sin

The Bible is filled with people experiencing all kinds of spiritual, emotional, relational, and mental difficulties – all of which are the residual effects of sin. Three Biblical examples are King David as narrated in 2 Samuel 11; Achan in the book of Joshua 7: 1-26 and Ananias and Sapphira in Acts 5: 1-11. Christians are not immune or exempt from the devastating impact of sin. According to His will, God then determines who to heal and how to heal. There are times when He will heal by supernatural means. Other times, God will choose to heal us through medication, surgery, or sharing of increased knowledge on human issues, which is where professional counseling comes in.

If you believe that you may have some unresolved issues that might be hindering your walk with God and your relationship with others, I strongly recommend that you seek out a professional Christian counselor. Some issues limit or hinder our walk with God. Judas Iscariot is a perfect example. He was so close to Jesus and knew better! Yet, he found himself engaged in the sinful act of stealing money.

He had a compulsion that he was never able to conquer. He suggested they could have used the money spent anointing

Jesus to buy food for the poor – yet he stole from the money box. He could have confessed his weakness to Jesus or others. He could have sought help to deal with his financial issues appropriately. His unhealthy desires for money and failure to seek help resulted in Satan filling his heart to sell or betray Jesus for money, 30 pieces of silver. This is a stunning example for those who have unresolved weaknesses and fail to seek help from God, His word, and others – professional Christian counselors.

CHAPTER 8
A Spiritual Approach to Counseling

Taking a spiritual approach to counseling doesn't guarantee success, but that doesn't mean Christians shouldn't look into the values and beliefs of a counselor before beginning therapy. While we don't necessarily look for Christian plumbers or auto mechanics, psychological care is different.

"There's such an interface between the Christian faith and what goes on in the counseling room," says Sanders. "One of the primary areas in which that is true is the issue of values. An example might be the couple who comes in and is interested in getting some marital counseling. How will the counselor respond after they hear the nature of the problems? Some counselors are much more ready to hit the divorce button if they hear different things, but you're much less likely to hear that from a Christian counselor. Research shows that clients will feel better toward a counselor when they know the counselor shares their values. So, when possible, I would say that people should seek out a counselor that shares their faith values."

Doug Trouten, the President of the Evangelical Press Association, said it this way. "Shouldn't Christians be able to solve all their problems through prayer, Bible study, and counseling with pastors and other mature Christians? The spiritual truths of the Bible – salvation, forgiveness, and spiritual healing through our Savior, Jesus Christ – transcend all ages. Yet changes in society since the Bible was written have created problems that are not extensively addressed in the Bible. Some problems require help from a counselor with specialized training."

Here is another statement that you may also hear. "Other people can handle their problems, so if I just try harder, won't I be able to handle my problems too?" Comparing yourself with how others seem to be coping is not fair to yourself. Emotional problems are often deeply rooted in our past and can also be biologically induced. None of us share the same past experiences, and we do not have the same abilities to cope with problems. You may need help handling problems that others can deal with on their own.

CHAPTER 9
The Power of Prayer and Counseling

Prayer and counseling? The Prophet Nehemiah gave us some sound Biblical counsel. In Nehemiah 1:1–3, while in Persia, Nehemiah was visited by his brethren from Judah and enquired about his homeland. His brother reported that [3] "They said to me, 'Things are not going well for those who returned to the province of Judah. They are in great trouble and disgrace. The wall of Jerusalem has been torn down, and the gates have been destroyed by fire.' [4] When I heard this, I sat down and wept. In fact, for days I mourned, fasted, and prayed to the God of heaven."

In Chapter 2, Nehemiah goes to Jerusalem to begin rebuilding the wall in Chapter 3. However, in Chapter 4, his enemies oppose him from every side. Verse 9 is very interesting. It states that they prayed but did something after that. They placed guards at every vulnerable area of the work. What we see here is prayer backed up by taking action.

Nehemiah could have said, "Well, we have prayed; go home, relax. God will take care of us." They believed God would protect and give them victory over their enemies, but there was no excuse for not exercising their faith through action. We will also discover this in verse 14. Nehemiah essentially told his people to fight for their families.

In this light, we can also fight for our families by seeking professional help for personal, emotional, relational, and spiritual issues that we and our loved ones are struggling with.

Professional Christian counseling helps us in the following ways:

- Identify our hurts, pains, struggles, and wounds.
- Understand the relationship of the spirit, soul, and body.
- Show us how our childhood experiences can impact or influence our adult life.
- Show us how God has called and equipped others to provide the emotional support and resources available to the body of Christ to help bring wholeness.

Based upon the reactions I have gotten from many Christians on the mention of professional Christian counseling, a majority tend to evade, avoid, or ignore such recommendations. They say they do not want anyone to 'mess with their minds.' The harsh reality is that our minds have been 'messed up' due to our sinful nature.

Aren't most of our battles fought in our minds? The meaning of repentance is to 'change one's mind.' The mind affects how we think, which affects how we feel, and how we behave.

The battle for the mind is also the battle for the soul. Our minds have been impacted by the fall. Sin has disrupted and tainted the soul. Some theologians believe the conversation between Eve and the devil was not physical and verbal, but mental and psychological. Others believe that the serpent that walked upright before the curse possessed enough intelligence to express itself in words. The devil used the serpent as a tool.

Sanders said: "It has been suggested that just as the speaking of Balaam's ass was a divine miracle, so the speaking of the serpent was a diabolical miracle." Whichever explanation suits you, we can conclude that the senses of sight, touch, and taste were involved. There was also thought processing, reasoning, and decision-making. We can see here that the soul of Eve was troubled and eventually fell to sin. The soul that sin shall die. That soulish decision to eat impacted her spirit, leading to spiritual death or separation from God. This spiritual death eventually led to physical death, which we all will experience. One can again see how we are both tripartite and triune beings. The devil is an intelligent, spiritual being – though extremely wicked. So, in his enmity against God because of his judgment, he is committed to destroying God's prime creation, man, by whatever means necessary.

This is what happened in the Garden of Eden. Eve changed her mind from obeying God, who said do not eat of this fruit, to obeying the devil, who said you would not die if you eat of the fruit. That was a one-eighty-degree decision that cost man his dominion on earth and the miracle of living forever at ease.

2 Corinthians 11:3 (NKJV) says, "But I fear, lest somehow,

as the serpent deceived Eve by his craftiness, so your minds may be corrupted from the simplicity that is in Christ."

As mentioned before, sin has negatively impacted animals and nature in general. However, all that was lost through sin can now be regained through the shed blood of Jesus' death on the Cross. However, man has to change back his mind about following Christ because the damaging effects of the original sin still impact him. It is very interesting that regarding the mind, the Bible says in Romans 12:2 (NLT), "Don't copy the behavior and customs of this world but let God transform you into a new person by changing the way you think. Then you will learn to know God's will for you, which is good and pleasing and perfect." Philippians 2:5 (NKJV) says, "Let this mind be in you which was also in Christ Jesus...". The battle in the mind is the battle for the soul. Satan knows that...

As Christians we must be aware of that and welcome, even applaud, the services of professional Christian counselors as agents whom God uses to help heal the mind and bring it into conformity to the will of God. What affects your mind affects your heart, which then affects your health and, ultimately, your life. The Apostle Paul said in Philippians 4:7 (KJV), "And the peace of God, which passeth all understanding, shall keep your hearts and minds through Christ Jesus."

I can say that the peace of God will rule your heart so that you do not get a heart attack and that the peace of God will rule your mind so that you will not go crazy. In other words, God gives peace to our souls.

Still dealing with the issue of the mind, we can also agree that one word can lead to a thought, and one thought can lead to a particular action or behavior, which, in turn, can be developed into a lifestyle. That lifestyle will eventually determine one's destiny. 2 Timothy 1:7 says, "For God has not given us a spirit of fear but of power and love and a sound mind."

CHAPTER 10
Secular Versus Christian Counseling

Professional Christian counseling is another God-given tool to help develop a sound mind. Let us explore some differences between Christian counseling and secular counseling.

In most cases, Christian and secular counseling share a common objective: to assist individuals in overcoming their challenges, discovering purpose and happiness in life, and achieving mental and emotional well-being. Most counselors hold advanced degrees and have dedicated years to sharpening their expertise.

"Christian and secular counselors might strive to help the individual overcome their problems, work through a crisis, deal with grief, attain mental/physical health, and become well-adjusted. Christian counselors, however, will also focus on helping the individual find Godly meaning in their life. They will strive to increase the individual's joy by helping them to form a stronger, closer relationship with God". Christian counselors know that people cannot fully heal unless they have a genuine and strong relationship with Christ.

Secular counselors claim to look at their clients as a whole, but this is impossible as long as they deny the spiritual aspect of individuals. Christian counselors are set apart from all others because they acknowledge that their clients are spiritual beings.

Secular counselors will examine why the individual is attending counseling and try to explain it using psychological constructs, theories, and ideas. Christian counselors will use these same constructs only after examining the individual's life in terms of where they might fall short in their walk with God.

Clients in Christian counseling will almost always encounter the same reasoning behind their problems. This reasoning states that the individual is failing to comply with the life guidelines in the Bible or they are not submitting to God's will. They will continue to struggle daily until they can fix those two things.

For the professional Christian counselor, the scriptures set up their practice guidelines. One scripture that can be described as the root of all Christian counseling is 2 Timothy 3:16–17 (NIV) which states, [16] "All Scripture is God-breathed and is useful for teaching, rebuking, correcting and training in righteousness, [17] so that the man of God may be thoroughly equipped for every good work." Christian counselors must match everything they say or do according to this scripture; otherwise, they are working outside God's will.

If you are a believer of the Bible, if you trust its word, regardless of whether you are Catholic, Baptist, Pentecostal, or any other denomination or religion, a Christian counselor can work for you because they use the word as it is written, with no exceptions. The Bible is today what it was yesterday and will be tomorrow. This means that professional Christian counselors never change the standard for treatment.

Secular counselors ride the waves of pop psychology, relying on the most recent research studies or theories created by men. The counselor is forced to move on to the newest fad when another man comes along and falsifies the first. Morals are important to most of us – even the most agnostic individuals will have morals that say it is OK to do certain things but not OK to do others.

When a counselor is licensed by the state, which makes them a professional counselor, the state has the right to tell the counselor what morals they have and what moral values they are allowed to impose on their patient. In other words, if you say that you are going to harm a family member the counselor would be allowed to report you and tell you that your decision is not good or wrong.

Whereas, if the individual was going to get an abortion, you could not say, one way or the other, whether the individual was right in doing so. According to the state, every choice is based on an individual's morals and values. The Christian counselor will also have their own values and guidelines for good practice including the appropriate utilization of Biblical principles.

Regarding Christian counseling, the amazing news is that people who pray live longer, are healthier, overcome more sickness and chronic illness, have fewer mental health problems, and are generally more prosperous and, happy.

Prayer has been proven more effective than counseling and medicine combined! Imagine if you combined prayer with professional Christian counseling and, when appropriate, with medication. It's a win, win, win!

CHAPTER 11
The Stigma Associated with Counseling

'Social stigma' is the fear that others will judge a person negatively if they seek help for a problem (Deane & Chamberlain, 1994). Research found the social stigma attached to seeking professional help to be one of the most significant barriers to treatment (Sibicky & Dovidio, 1986; Stefl & Prosperi, 1985). This may be because the public in general tends to provide negative descriptions of individuals who experience mental illness (Crisp, Gelder, Rix, Meltzer, & Rowlands, 2000).

A history of having sought outpatient mental health services can lead others to have more negative perceptions of the individual (Dovidio, Fishbane, & Sibicky, 1985), including being labeled more awkward, cold, defensive, dependent, insecure, sad, and unsociable (Sibicky & Dovidio, 1986), viewing that individual as less in control of her or his emotions (Oppenheimer & Miller, 1988), and describing the individual as weak or disturbed (King, Newton, Osterlund & Baber, 1973).

Some researchers have also found that being labeled a 'former mental hospital patient' led to greater social rejection than was true for someone with no such label (Link,

Cullen, Frank, & Wozniak, 1987). Society views people who experience depression as emotionally unstable. However, they view those who seek help for depression as particularly unstable (Ben-Porath, 2002). This suggests that it is not simply they are having a disorder but seeking help from a professional who is stigmatized. Perhaps it is not surprising that people seek help less for problems associated with greater negative judgments by others (Overbeck, 1977). Most of those who have been to therapy perceive social stigma associated with their having sought help (Sirey et al., 2001).

Research has indicated a direct link between perceived social stigma and the inclination to seek professional assistance. Studies have revealed that social stigma not only influences a person's attitudes toward seeking help but also impacts their future intentions to seek help (ne & Todd, 1996; Komiya et al., 2000; Vogel et al., 2005), as well as predicting their likelihood of seeking help at a later date (Deane & Chamberlain, 1994). For instance, Stef and Prosperi (1985) discovered that individuals in need of treatment who refrained from seeking therapy were twice as likely as those who sought treatment to identify stigma as a significant barrier to accessing treatment.

In addition, more than 90% of the sample in another study (Nelson & Barbaro, 1985) agreed that the fear that others may think them crazy was a potential barrier to seeking help. Finally, Rochlen, Mohr, and Hargrove (1999) found that the stigma associated with seeking help for career issues was associated with more negative attitudes toward counseling and less intent to seek help. Researchers (e.g., Tinsley et al., 1984) have suggested that individuals who do not seek counseling services may have lower expectations about the benefits of seeking help than those who seek such services.

Bayer and Peay (1997) also found that individuals who did not seek help for a problem were more likely to feel uncertain about whether they would benefit from seeking help. In examining the utility of career counseling, Rochlen et al. (1999) found that persons who perceived more value in seeking help for career issues were also more likely to report intent to go to counseling for career issues.

Similarly, Vogel and Wester (2003) found that the utility of and risks expected from seeking help strongly predicted attitudes toward seeking help. Furthermore, Vogel et al. (2005) found that utility generally predicted help-seeking behavior. In contrast, risk predicted help-seeking for those who had experienced a distressing event in their life. Thus, it seems that expectations may play a role in people's help-seeking decisions.

Self-disclosure – a barrier to treatment

Another avoidance factor may be an individual's comfort in disclosing distressing or personal information. Jourard (1964) first described how the ability to self-disclose to another is central to a person's decision to seek help because to be helped, the person must choose to reveal private feelings, thoughts, and attitudes to another person.

Since Jourard's study, several researchers have suggested that self-disclosure is important in a person's decision to seek help (Hinson & Swanson, 1993; Vogel & Wester, 2003; Vogel et al., 2005). Kelly and Achter (1995) and Cepeda-Benito and Short (1998), found that one's desire to conceal personal information is related to past help-seeking behavior and current help-seeking intentions.

Kelly and Achter found that high concealers reported fewer positive attitudes about seeking help. However, these individuals did report greater intentions to seek mental health services. Cepeda-Benito and Short found that self-concealment interacted with social support to predict help-seeking intentions. They also found that self-concealers were three times more likely to have not sought therapy when experiencing a problem.

Four additional studies also revealed a correlation between an individual's ease in sharing with a therapist and their attitudes and motivations for seeking help. Hinson and Swanson's research in 1993 found that the readiness of an individual to disclose their concerns to a counselor, in conjunction with the severity of their issue, had the most significant impact on their willingness to seek assistance.

Vogel and Wester (2003) and Vogel et al. (2005) found that one's comfort in disclosing distressing information was a unique predictor of attitudes and intent to seek help. They also found that self-disclosure was an even stronger predictor of help-seeking than self-concealment. Finally, Diala et al. (2000) reported that people uncomfortable talking about personal issues with a professional were five times less likely to seek help. A person's comfort with self-disclosure is a factor that an individual considers when deciding whether or not to seek help.

CHAPTER 12
How Is My Self-esteem?

Researchers have typically neglected the examination of self-esteem as a determining factor in an individual's choice to access counseling services. Nevertheless, self-esteem has been acknowledged as a significant psychological hurdle when seeking help from informal sources such as family and friends (Nadler, 1991). Fisher, Nadler, and Whitcher-Alagna (1982) proposed that seeking assistance from another involves an inherent assessment of the trade-offs between preserving one's self-esteem.

To some extent, turning to others for help implies recognizing that one cannot address the issue independently, potentially signifying a form of personal inadequacy (Fisher et al., 1982). Consequently, individuals might opt not to seek help to uphold a positive self-image (Miller, 1985). Several studies concerning informal help-seeking align with this notion. Instances of seeking help tend to be less frequent when embarrassment hinders the process (Shapiro, 1983), and self-esteem has shown a direct correlation with the general pursuit of assistance for issues described as significant (Bee-Gates, Howard-Pitney, Rowe, & LaFromboise, 1996).

Some cultures believe it's best to deal with problems by

not thinking about or dwelling on them, which doesn't align with the counselor's values of openly discussing feelings and emotions (Cheng, Leong, & Geist, 1993). In African-American culture, for instance, there is an emphasis on facing difficulties with strength and endurance (Broman, 1996).

Race and ethnicity

The impact of cultural values on seeking help is crucial, especially in cultures with strong social networks. In these cultures, counselors might be considered outsiders who aren't part of the close-knit social circle or family (Atkinson et al., 1990; Yeh, 2002). Consequently, many minority groups turn to family and friends for help rather than seeking counseling assistance.

For instance, Mexican-American and African-American youth tend to rely on family members more often than American youth when facing issues (Offer, Howard, Schonert, & Ostriv, 1991). Likewise, compared to European Americans, Japanese Americans are more inclined to seek help from family and friends rather than therapists (Narikiyo & Kameoka, 1992). Various factors such as acculturation, cultural identity, cultural mistrust, and cultural commitment have been associated with attitudes toward seeking help, tolerance for the stigma attached to seeking help, and willingness to discuss problems with a counselor (Atkinson et al., 1990; Tata & Leong, 1994; Nickerson, Helms, & Terrell, 1994; Price & McNeill, 1992). Additionally, increasing an individual's confidence in counseling and the counselor's credibility has been linked to seeking help (Dadfar & Friedlander, 1982) and reducing avoidance factors (Akutsu, Lin, & Zane, 1990).

In some cultures, seeking help outside the family is considered shameful or damaging to one's reputation (Cheong & Snowden, 1990). Worries about how seeking services might affect one's family can deter someone from seeking professional help (Root, 1985). Therefore, understanding the impact of labeling and stigma on different racial groups is essential (Diala et al., 2000). Moreover, the ease of seeking help can vary depending on the type of counseling needed. Seeking help for certain types of counseling may be worse than it is for other types.

The stigma associated with career counseling may be less than that for personal counseling, particularly for individuals from some cultures (Leong, 1993). In summary, the potential role that race and ethnicity have in influencing help-seeking avoidance is significant.

CHAPTER 13
What Am I afraid Of?

Treatment fears, apprehension, and concerns about counseling can lead people to avoid therapy (Kushner & Sher, 1989). As a reminder, professional counselors' goal is to reduce these concerns of potential clients by correcting the negative perceptions surrounding seeking counseling services. In particular, professional counselors need to directly challenge inaccurate myths about therapy and educate potential clients about the counseling process. Researchers have suggested that people often do not know much about professional counseling or psychotherapy (Jorm, 2000). They often base their perceptions on inaccurate information from media or other sources (Crisp et al., 2000).

Very often, the fears of potential clients about counseling services represent a mixture of what they have heard about counselors, social workers, mental health workers, psychologists, or psychiatrists because frequently, the general public does not distinguish between the responsibilities of these professional groups. Therefore, we need to discuss fears about being medicated, hospitalized, or otherwise controlled directly.

Let's talk about the 'fear of negative affect.' Because

counseling is often seen as involving an emotional interaction, people may fear having to experience painful effects (Komiya et al., 2000). One way to combat this fear is to dispel some common myths about counseling. People may think that the counselor will force them to tell all their deepest thoughts, feelings, and secrets to the therapist or that they will be 'put on the hot seat.' In seeking professional counseling, you control what, how much, and when to share emotional information. Professional Christian counseling is about helping the individual live a healthier life than what they may be experiencing before walking into the office.

In his book, *Biblical Concepts for Christian Counseling*, William T. Kirwan asserted that there are four basic counseling positions related to Christianity and psychology.[1]

- The first view is called the '**unchristian view**.' Proponents of this view insist that religion, more so Biblical Christianity, has nothing to offer individuals. The unchristian view assumes that human reason is the ultimate source of truth. The Bible refutes such statements since it is clearly stated that Jesus is the way, the truth, and the light. All truth is, therefore, God's truth, and if a human is the ultimate source of truth, that makes the human God, which is idolatry.

- The second counseling position is the '**spiritualized view**,' which believes that revelation supersedes reason and may be contrary to reason. According to this view, all emotional disturbances result from man violating God's law. Here, they limit themselves to spiritual truths, ignoring or failing to recognize that other truths are also God's truth. Although Christians believe that the Bible has the answers to man's meaning and purpose in life, it is imperative to remember that it is not a medical textbook. One truth is that human beings have been divinely gifted with the ability to develop and use the science of medicine. Certain psychological and physical laws are part of our makeup. We cannot ignore them as though they are irrelevant to our well-being. We must go beyond pure spiritual teaching to understand that. To believe that anger, mental distress, depression, and anxiety are always the result of disobedience or some conscious sin you harbor is unfair to the person experiencing those psycho-emotional deficits. Those issues could have come about from the sins of others.

- The third view is called the '**parallel view.**' It accepts both reason and revelation to be relevant in counseling. In this view, counselors hold to a firm Christian position and, at the same time, make use of psychological findings. In their counseling, such persons use God's truth as revealed in scripture and scientific principles of psychology and counseling. However, those counselors keep scripture and psychology separate. Here many counselors fail to recognize that God gave man the ability to study his behavior as one of his many bestowed gifts.

- Finally, the '**integrated view**' blends scripture with psychology. Since God is the author of both Revelation (Bible) and reason (psychology), all truth is ultimately part of a unified or integrated whole (Carter (1977),

- 204). The integrated view speaks not only about the Bible concerning sin and salvation but also about God's mandate for us to replenish and have dominion over the earth. To fulfill this mandate, we must learn all we can about his handiwork, including ourselves. A good professional Christian counselor will emphasize God's providence, sovereignty and, active relevance in all of His creation, alongside the good news of salvation. Although all problems are due to the universality of sin, those who hold to the integrated view point out that some psychological problems do not result from individual or conscious sin. Although, in principle, all sickness, be it physical, spiritual, or emotional, is rooted in sin, one should differentiate personal conscious sin and the inherited sinfulness that taints everything.

By virtue of the fall, all of us are in bondage to sin. However, personal sin is not necessarily the cause of emotional difficulties. In dealing with the issue of Christianity and psychology, it is clear that scripture designated human beings as spirit, soul, and body. God's word does not compartmentalize personhood but presents a holistic view of human nature. The Christian, therefore, must be careful to view the total person as God's creation. William T. Kirwan states that psychological laws are integral to the creation order itself and are assumed everywhere in the Bible. He also says that throughout scripture, there is a stress on the human need for relationships and that the Bible is embedded with data on the chief dimensions of the human personality – knowing, being, and doing. These statements, therefore, mean that

God's word does not regard psychology as useless.

When dealing with human needs, we can integrate psychological and theological truths. God has given man the ability to create unimaginable inventions and technologies. He also gives man the ability to develop medication and treat diseases, including mental health problems. This is all part of what the Bible tells us about the increase of man's knowledge. Daniel 12:4 (NLT) says, "But you, Daniel, keep this prophecy a secret; seal up the book until the time of the end, when many will rush here and there, and knowledge will increase."

CHAPTER 14
The Impact of Eden

W e can see in God's creation the application of
foundational laws that impacted land, vegetation,
animals, and man. Some of those include the laws of physics,
chemistry, astrology, geology, and biology. Keeping
psychology in the mix, we can say that the law of psychology
investigates the physical causes and correlates of behavior and
emotions, and includes the law of physiology. The law of
physiology builds on and includes the laws of biology and
chemistry.

Therefore, the study of chemistry is crucial to a complete
understanding of psychology, including sexual identity, self-
image, and conditions such as schizophrenia, psychosomatic
illness, and depression. Regarding Christianity, the spiritual
laws that govern us, are not to be equated with but do include
psychology, biology, and chemical laws. In discussing human
beings, the Bible does assume those physical and biological
laws essential to the definition of human beings. The study of
psychology, which is a God-created category, is legitimate and
proper, providing that one remembers that it is part of a larger
whole. The spiritual laws governing humans encompass far
more than psychology.

The Bible never denies or ignores the importance of the physical and biological dimensions of the human person. Jesus ate, got tired, and slept, and Paul's concerns for Timothy's ailments reflected biological realities. The Bible also is clear on the importance of interpersonal relationships. In Genesis 2:18, God said it is not good for man to be alone. This tells us that Adam needed human companionship to experience, social intimacy, happiness, and satisfaction. For this purpose, God created Eve. Even before the fall, God singled out the social needs of the individual as very important. After the fall, the need for close relationships increased, and that which remained became severely distorted. Through the fall, Adam tainted the destiny of all mankind through procreation. One of the results of the fall is mental and emotional suffering – psychopathology.

From Genesis 2–3 and Romans 1, we can observe three things:

- God has created us to have spiritual and social needs.
- A good relationship with God and others is necessary to fulfill those needs.
- If our needs are not met by good or healthy interpersonal relationships, we become spiritually, psychologically, and emotionally disoriented, just like Adam.

"One of the consequences of sin is a loss of sense of belonging, resulting in the negative emotions of anxiety and insecurity. There was also a loss of self-esteem, with human feelings of guilt and shame, and also a loss of strength, resulting in feelings of depression and helplessness".

The fall stripped us of our God image. Because of Jesus' blood, we can be a new creation and again have the image we had before the fall. God warned Adam and Eve that if they disobeyed him, they will surely die. Their sin affected them spiritually, physically, and psychologically. Because of the fall, mankind now suffers from bodily disorders, deformities, abnormalities, and deterioration. Bodily diseases not only include cardiovascular problems or crippled limbs, but also physical problems that are related to emotional suffering.

In reference to the creation story, "Adam and Eve would have experienced a sense of rejection, alienation, weakness, a sense of shame, and guilt to the point where they 'hid their face from God.' They lost their original relationship with God. Those deficits created what would now be innate mental, emotional, relational, and spiritual issues which have become part of the human experiences and struggles today".

Those who seek professional Christian counseling would admit that, in one way or another, their mental, emotional, and relational struggles harm their spiritual or Christian life. This is because, in reality, we cannot separate body, soul, and spirit from each other. They consist of one person, as the Godhead, three in one. Gleaning from the Edenic experience, we can also say that spiritual counseling edifies and strengthens one's spirit or Christian life as it relates to (God/Bible). Physical counseling strengthens one's body as it relates to (a physician), and emotional counseling strengthens one's heart and soul as it relates to (a professional Christian counselor).

CHAPTER 15
Removing Whatever Hinders

A professional Christian counselor is a member of God's family and family members help each other according to their abilities, capacity, and giftedness. The Bible says in Romans 15:2 (NLT), "We should help others do what is right and build them up in the Lord." 1 Thessalonians 5:11 (NLT) says, "So encourage each other and build each other up, just as you are already doing."

One of the goals of building up others is to help them gain a comprehensive understanding of themselves and develop an objective, healthy, and integrated perspective of their problems or issues and how these can impact their lives and their relationship with other people and the world. This process will help them to see the need to make positive changes in their lives.

As a counselee begins to view themselves objectively, the counselor can help them identify and apply unused resources to their lives, especially Biblical doctrine. This will result in significant positive change and enhance their identity and functioning in Christ. "One of the purposes of counseling is to find ways of solving past or current problems and being equipped with the tools to deal with future issues". Christians are called and commanded to serve one another.

Professional Christian counseling brings a person to a productive and improved place in their life to a point, where that person, in turn, can better serve God and others. Christian counseling allows people to adequately handle the personal, emotional, relational, and spiritual dimensions of their lives. It can help bring you to a place where self-destructive behavioral patterns can no longer hold you hostage or encumbered and where more of your positive resources can be discovered and utilized.

One of the benefits of professional Christian counseling is exploring or attempting to trace or identify the root of the problem. The total of a person's childhood experiences can bring about a certain personality and character structure. According to (Horney 1945, 41), some of the elements that can impact one's childhood are domination by parents, indifference, erratic treatment, lack of respect for the child's individual needs, lack of real guidance, disparaging attitude, too much admiration (or its absence), lack of encouragement and warmth from parents, too much or too little responsibility, overprotection, isolation of parents from their children, injustice, discrimination, unkept promises, hostile atmosphere, quarrelsome parents, etc. These factors can leave a child feeling insecure, anxious, and helpless in a potentially hostile world. Horney says that the past, in some way or other, is always contained in the present.

Stop reading right now and take some time to reflect on how it was for you growing up in your family of origin. You may be surprised (or not surprised) to realize how much your present adult life has been in some way impacted by some things you have experienced as a child. The truth is that an emotionally wounded person can become an emotionally healed Christian. However, this may not always be the case because of the type, depth, and impact of the wounds and one's willingness to do the hard work in professional counseling to get there.

In situations like this, born-again believers may require spiritual and emotional counseling to experience the level of healing that would equip them to live a productive life. The fact is that both mental and emotional disorders are among the serious consequences of the fall. As such, we should address these so that the image of God can be restored in his children. I believe redemption involves not only reconciliation with God but a healing of mental pathology. If someone claims to be a Christian but their behavioral pattern is plagued with inconsistencies, that situation should be explored to clear up any dysfunction that is hampering their walk with God.

I strongly believe that sin has had and still is presently having a devastating impact on the human psyche/heart. I do not believe that for everyone mental/emotional healing comes automatically at the point of salvation and that there may be some lingering issues that one may need to address through counseling as they grow in their faith journey, which can be described as progressive sanctification.

Some theologians believe in the 'accomplishment of redemption' and the 'application of redemption.' The accomplishment of redemption concerns Jesus' once for all purchase of our redemption when He died on the cross. On the other hand, is the application of redemption that concerns our personal experience of salvation. Consistent with the theology of salvation, we must remember that salvation begins in the heart. As we live out our lives, it will be completed when we are glorified with Christ in eternity.

This means that the process of our salvation is extensive, thorough, and continuing. As believers, before we can move to a place of affirmation and approval in Christ, we must first experience the calling, regeneration, conversion, and justification that impacts our mental and emotional state. Becoming a Christian does not make us immune to having feelings. Our feelings can range from joy to sadness, hurt to heal, shy to shame, insecure to guilt, accepted to rejected, love to hate, and anger to forbearance. Some of those negative emotions can have an unhealthy effect on one's interpersonal relationships. In Christian counseling, we can address such issues to help the individual grow and develop healthier relationships. Sanctification is the gradual process of change within the believer. We become more and more like Christ through the daily inner workings of the Holy Spirit.

The Apostle Paul talks about putting off the old man and putting on the new man in Ephesians 4:21–24 (NLT), [21] "Since you have heard about Jesus and have learned the truth that comes from him, [22] throw off your old sinful nature and your former way of life, which is corrupted by lust and deception. [23] Instead, let the Spirit renew your thoughts and attitudes. [24] Put on your new nature, created to be like God – truly righteous and holy."

Some things we need to put off would include bad habits, attitudes, negative behaviors, etc. Because we are creatures of habit, we tend to repeat the past and hold on to our illusions. We find our security in what is familiar, even when it may be destructive or dysfunctional. Professional Christian counseling helps us explore those issues and develop ways to become healthier. As Christians, until our lives on earth are over, there will be ongoing issues that will require our attention, and need to seek support.

I am wondering what your thoughts will be after reading through this book. Would it impact you in a way that has you thinking that professional Christian counseling will benefit you or someone you deeply love or care about? The next chapter addresses clarifying terms, questions, and answers from Steve

W. Patrick, PsyD, which will be of additional help to you and your loved ones.

CHAPTER 16
Frequently Asked Questions About Counseling

What's the difference between a psychiatrist and a psychologist?

A psychiatrist has an MD degree (Doctor of Medicine) or DO (Doctor of Osteopathy) and has chosen to specialize in the branch of medicine that focuses on mental health issues. A psychiatrist treats patients by talking with them and prescribing medication (if needed). Psychologists have one of these degrees: Ph.D. (Doctor of Philosophy), PsyD (Doctor of Psychology), or EdD (Doctor of Education). A psychologist treats patients by talking with them but does not prescribe medication. (If medication is needed, a psychologist will refer the patient to an MD such as a psychiatrist, a family physician, or another type of MD.)

What's the difference between the terms 'counseling,' 'therapy,' and 'psychotherapy'?

In one sense, there are no differences since they all imply that you talk to a mental health professional to help solve various problems in your life. In another sense, there is a significant difference. The term 'counseling' is a short-term and very focused approach to solving the client's problems. The term 'psychotherapy' means a long-term and more in-depth approach.

The term 'therapy' is simply an abbreviated version of the term 'psychotherapy.'

What's the difference between a counselor, therapist, psychotherapist, psychologist, psychiatrist, social worker, marriage and family therapist, etc.?

At a basic level, there are no differences in that all mental health professionals talk to clients to help them solve their problems. At another level, significant differences in education and training can impact the type of help you receive. For instance, typically, the terms 'psychotherapist,' 'psychologist,' and 'psychiatrist' denote practitioners with a doctoral level of training. In contrast, the other terms denote practitioners with a master's level of training. But what determines how much a client resolves their problems while in treatment lies more within the client than the therapist.

Can't I just talk to someone I know who's a good listener and get the same help that I would from a therapist?

The following quote answers that question with a resounding 'No.' "... The bottom line is that patients want and need someone that listens to them. They want a therapist who can listen to them in depth. That is what we offer: We listen to people in depth, over an extended period, and with great intensity. We listen to what they say and don't say, to what they say in words and to what they say through their bodies and enactments. And we listen to them by listening to ourselves, our minds, our reveries, and our bodily reactions.

We listen to their life stories and to the story that they live with us in the room; their past, their present, and future. We listen to what they already know or can see about themselves, and we listen to what they can't see in themselves. We listen to ourselves listening. Whatever managed care says, and whatever drugs are prescribed, and whatever the research findings, people still want to be listened to in-depth and always will." (Aron, 2009).

How can you fix a problem by only talking about it?

This question tells us a lot about the culture we live in today. We are action-oriented and usually want to know several action steps that we can take to solve our problems. Patiently thinking or talking about a given problem seems ridiculous and a waste of time. But truly meaningful, significant change must begin from within, and changing from within requires a shift in perspective (a paradigm shift). This, in turn, usually happens only after contemplating an issue for a while and after talking to caring others and feeling the strength of their support.

Will my psychologist/counselor think I'm weird, crazy, or sick?

In a word, no. Anyone who enters psychotherapy is courageous and should be respected because they are doing something about their problems by facing and confronting them.

How long will I be in treatment?

In general, a circumscribed issue with a short history will probably be dealt with fairly quickly, for example, in 10 to 20 sessions. However, a non-specific issue with a long history like, "I've never really been a happy person," will probably need much longer to be dealt with, say six months to several years.

Will I be sent to a mental hospital against my will?

No, this does not happen to most people. Very few instances would dictate hospitalization, namely, only when safety issues are a concern. Out of the general population, only a very small percentage ever needs to be hospitalized for psychological reasons, and even fewer are taken against their will. (Again, these few have to threaten harm to themselves or someone else.)

Will I fall apart if I start talking about upsetting thoughts and feelings?

For most people, the answer is no, at least not in terms of a 'nervous breakdown' or crying uncontrollably. It is certainly possible that you may cry or feel anxious or upset. But many people feel relief after letting their feelings out during a session.

Am I a failure if I go to a counselor, therapist, or psychologist?

No, I do not believe this to be true. However, the answer depends upon whom you listen to. Unfortunately, many in our society still view a visit to a mental health provider as a sign of some inherent weakness or deficiency in the person. The good news is that many others see this view as outdated and even foolish.

I suggest consulting a mental health provider be viewed the same as when one visits another professional, for example, a physician. On the one hand, we could say someone has a physical weakness if they get the flu and have to visit their physician. On the other hand, we could say that person is wise to seek the help of a trained professional. I believe it is the same for an emotional or behavioral problem; that is, it is wise (not weak) to seek professional help.

Can't I just read a book, attend a support group, etc., and get the help I need?

You can try that, but you may have already tried several methods. From my experience, most of my clients have already tried several avenues to deal with their problems by the time they come in for psychotherapy. The problem I hear over and over is that the self-help book, seminar, support group, etc., that the client utilized was not specific enough to their particular situation. In psychotherapy, we can discuss problems and the application of solutions to those problems in great detail.

Can't I just put my problems behind me, move on, and hope for the best next time?

You can certainly try that, but it often doesn't work if we are honest with ourselves. The more we deal with life in that manner, the more difficult it is to move on after each successive disappointment, frustration, or conflict. I think this is because each issue or situation that isn't dealt with appropriately accumulates with other prior unresolved issues. Then when too many issues accumulate, the overflow comes out in the form of symptoms like stress, anxiety, depression, irritability, lack of focus, stomach upset, headaches, muscle tightness, and the like. It is akin to a container that becomes too full and spills over if not monitored.

How do I know if I need to see a mental health provider?

One way to answer this question is to continue with the above metaphor. That is, you need to see a mental health provider when the container gets too full and strategies aimed at helping don't work. For example, you may find that talking to a friend or reading a self-help book doesn't improve things. Other indicators that you might want to see a professional include: you know the problem is too big or complex to handle easily; others suggest you need to talk to someone or get help; you've tried numerous strategies over the years and have had some success with the issue, but no real lasting or deep changes have occurred; or, you just don't seem to be reaching your full potential in your spiritual life, social, marriage, career, friendships, hobbies, etc.

How do I select a Christian counselor?

The key criteria for selecting a Christian counselor involve the counselor's credentials and faith. Just because a person refers to himself as a counselor does not necessarily mean he/she is properly trained. A counselor should be licensed by the state in which they practice. Also, if you are experiencing marriage problems, you may want to look for a Marriage and Family Therapist. MFTs have specific training in relationship dynamics. Licensed Professional Counselors (LPCs) have specific training in dealing with individual problems, but many also have experience and training in marital issues. You may also look for someone who has specific experience in working with couples in crisis.

Here are some questions to ask that will help you decide if a particular therapist is a good fit for you:

- What type of license do they have? The most common types of licensures include Licensed Professional Counselor (LPC), Licensed Marriage and Family Therapist (LMFT), Psychologist, Licensed Clinical Social Worker (LCSW), and Psychiatrist (MD).

- Where is the license held? Which state? The license should be from a state licensing board, not simply from a professional or national counseling association. The counselor's license should also be from the state where the therapist is currently working, not just from any state.

- Is their degree from an accredited university?

- What other credentials do they hold? Professional memberships?

- Do they have specific experience in working with couples in crisis? What type of problems have they worked with?

- Are they active or committed in their faith and

religious organization?

Just because a person refers to themselves as a Christian therapist does not necessarily mean that he/she is Christian in beliefs and practices. Here are some questions to help determine a Christian therapist's level of faith:

- Is he/she recognized and recommended by the local church community?

- Does he/she attend church regularly? What activities are they involved with at church? Does he/she teach a class or participate in service activities?

- Who is their minister or pastor? Does the counselor feel uncomfortable with the prospect of you talking to her pastor?

- Does the counselor have a statement of faith? Do their beliefs or does he/she beliefs conflict with you?

- What does the counselor believe about marriage, divorce and abortion, etc.?

- Does he/she encourage reconciliation and offer therapeutic services to couples toward that end?

- Does the counselor use prayer and Scripture in his/her practice?

If a counselor seems reluctant or uncomfortable in answering these questions, feel free to seek other recommendations from trusted Christian advisors such as church leaders, staff, Sunday school teachers, denominational boards, etc.

Focus on the Family offers a free referral service to over

2,000 licensed therapists who are screened and evaluated for their beliefs, expertise, and ethical practices.

CHAPTER 17
Your First Counseling Session

O n your first visit, your counselor will greet you either through online/telehealth or in-person office visit.

Telehealth counseling has become more popular since the pandemic. The availability of mental health services has become more convenient and flexible in the form of telehealth. Telehealth is a medium where you can have counseling services without going into an office. You can meet with your counselor online from the comfort of your home or anywhere else as long as you can access internet service on your computer, tablet, or smartphone. Through telehealth, all your intake documents are electronically completed and signed by you. The Health Insurance Portability and Accountability Act (HIPAA) ensures the safety, protection, and confidentiality of all your information.

After filling out the paperwork, the counselor will seek to make sure you are comfortable. The counselor will answer any questions you have, and then they will ask questions to get to know more about you.

As a result of being very interested in hearing your story, the counselor will ask you questions such as, "What brings you to see me for counseling today?" or "What are you seeking help for today?"

The counselor may ask questions while you are sharing your issues to clarify for greater understanding. The counselor will want to understand the difficulties you are experiencing and to prioritize them in order of importance. Before ending the first session, there will be a discussion of how many sessions it may take to attain your goal, the length of each session, the payment involved, and some form of contract. The number of sessions you may need depends on your presenting issues. Some sessions can take 3-4 weeks to 3, 6, or 9 months. Sometimes an individual can be in therapy for years depending on their presenting issues or problems. As pertaining to Christian counseling, these sessions most likely will begin and end with prayer. Then the counselor will schedule the next appointment. Usually, in the beginning stages of counseling, as there is progression and a renegotiation of the contract, sessions can be biweekly or monthly. Payments for service can be before or after each session.

Confidentiality in Counseling

Will what I say in counseling/therapy sessions be private and confidential?

Whatever you say or discuss in therapy sessions will be kept confidential. However, there are circumstances under which exceptions exist. A few exceptions where the counselor can break confidentiality include:

- If you are a threat to harm yourself or someone else.

- Child abuse or neglect is suspected.

- Your treatment records are requested by subpoena.

Who usually seeks counseling?

"The myth of only crazy people and people who can't handle life needed counseling"

Most people who come to counseling are normal people with issues, problems, or goals. People may see counseling in the following circumstances:

- If they want support, guidance, skills, or steps to meet personal goals.

- If they know some things from their past are holding them back from reaching their true potential.

- If they want their marriage to be better and more satisfying.

- If they are having normal relationships, careers, or personal issues that are making them feel unloved or depressed.

- If they are feeling anxious, experiencing sleeping difficulties and panic attacks, resulting in the inability to function properly at home, school, or work.

Fees How much does counseling cost?

The cost of professional counseling varies depending on different factors.

1. Insurance: Some insurance companies cover mental health counseling which is called outpatient behavioral health. Please check with

your insurance company to know what their benefits are. If you don't have insurance, you may be able to get free or low-cost mental health services through some professional organizations. Depending on income, you may be eligible for Medicaid which is a Federal program.

2. Out-of-Pocket Expense: This is a direct cost of service that you will have to pay which may include deductibles, coinsurance, and copayments that are not covered by your insurance company.

3. Sliding Scale Fee: This payment is for those who do not have insurance and want to pay for mental health services in cash. Among other things, the sliding scale is determined by income and family size. Therapy sessions vary from 45-60 minutes.

How can I get the most out of my counseling sessions?

In some counseling sessions, your counselor will give self-help assignments to be completed outside of the session. To maximize these self-help assignments, you are encouraged to work on the assignments and bring them into the counseling session with questions. In order to be successful, one must be active and take charge of their progress. When you are excited about the changes that you are making, you will have better success and see greater progress. Schedule a time daily usually around 15 minutes to practice the skills learned in the session.

If necessary, take notes in the sessions if you have difficulty retaining what was discussed. When not in counseling sessions, keep a personal journal writing things down that can then be discussed in the next session.

In the following six chapters, you can read more about common mental health issues. The information is not intended for you to diagnose yourself but rather to provide knowledge and understanding of some symptoms that you might be experiencing. It also includes some effective treatment approaches to help address those mental health issues.

CHAPTER 18
Anxiety Disorders

Anxiety is a normal reaction to stress and can be beneficial in some situations. For example, when one is faced with danger and anxiety, they will be more cautious or like preparing for a job interview or an important examination which will serve as a motivation to study for those occasions. For some, however, anxiety can become excessive and overwhelming. The person suffering may realize the feeling of anxiousness is harmful. They may also experience difficulty in controlling their feelings. Anxiety can negatively affect the day- to -day living such as job performance, school, work, and relationships.

There is a variety of anxiety disorders:

- Generalized Anxiety Disorder (GAD).

- Obsessive-Compulsive Disorder (OCD).

- Panic Disorder.

- Post-traumatic Stress Disorder (PTSD).

- Social Phobia (or Social Anxiety Disorder).

Collectively, they are among the most common mental disorders experienced by Americans.

Signs and symptoms

Anxiety disorders differ from regular, short-lived anxiety when facing stress, like public speaking or on a first date. These disorders stick around for at least six months and can worsen if you don't get help. They come with various symptoms, but they all revolve around having too much irrational fear and worry. If you think you might have an anxiety disorder, it's essential to seek help from a professional.

Anxiety disorders often show up alongside other mental or physical health issues, like alcohol or substance abuse, which can hide or make anxiety symptoms worse. Sometimes, these other problems need to be treated before the anxiety disorder.

Suitable treatments are available for anxiety disorders, and research is discovering new ways to help most people with these disorders live happy, productive lives. If you suspect you have an anxiety disorder, don't hesitate to seek information and treatment.

Around 40 million adults in the United States, aged 18 and older experience anxiety disorders each year, which makes them feel scared and uncertain.

Facts

- Anxiety disorders affect about 40 million American adults aged 18 years and older (about 18%) in a given year, causing them to feel fearful and uncertain.
- Women are 60% more likely than men to experience an anxiety disorder over their lifetime.
- Non-Hispanic blacks are 20% less likely, and Hispanics

are 30% less likely, than non-Hispanic whites to experience an anxiety disorder during their lifetime.

- An extensive national survey of adolescent mental health reported that about 8 percent of teens aged 13–18 have an anxiety disorder, with symptoms commonly emerging around age 6. However, of these teens, only 18 percent received mental health care.

Diagnosis

A medical doctor, psychologist, social worker, and mental health clinician must conduct a careful diagnostic evaluation to determine whether an anxiety disorder or a physical problem causes a person's symptoms. If the doctor diagnoses an anxiety disorder, they must also identify the type of disorder or the combination of disorders. The doctor should also identify coexisting conditions, such as depression or substance abuse. Sometimes alcoholism, depression, or other coexisting conditions strongly affect the individual. In such circumstances, treatment of the anxiety disorder must wait until the coexisting conditions are brought under control. (Source: National Institutes of Health)

CHAPTER 19
Attention Deficit Hyperactivity Disorder (ADHD, ADD)

ADHD, also known as Attention Deficit Hyperactivity Disorder or ADD, is a widespread childhood condition that can persist into teenage years and even adulthood. It involves challenges in maintaining focus, staying attentive, controlling behavior, and managing hyperactivity.

According to the Diagnostic Statistical Manual, 5th Edition (DSM-5), Attention-Deficit/Hyperactivity Disorder has three subtypes: Individuals with ADHD show a persistent pattern of inattention and/or hyperactivity-impulsivity that interferes with functioning or development:

1. Inattention: Six or more symptoms of inattention for children up to age 16 years, or five or more for adolescents age 17 years and older and adults; symptoms of inattention have been present for at least 6 months, and they are inappropriate for developmental level:

- Often fails to give close attention to details or makes careless mistakes in schoolwork, at work, or with other activities.

- Often has trouble holding attention on tasks or play activities.

- Often does not seem to listen when spoken to directly.

- Often does not follow through on instructions and fails to finish schoolwork, chores, or duties in the workplace (e.g., loses focus, side-tracked).

- Often has trouble organizing tasks and activities.

- Often avoids, dislikes, or is reluctant to do tasks that require mental effort over a long period of time (such as schoolwork or homework).

- Often loses things necessary for tasks and activities (e.g. school materials, pencils, books, tools, wallets, keys, paperwork, eyeglasses, mobile telephones).

- Is often easily distracted.

- Is often forgetful in daily activities.

    1. Hyperactivity and Impulsivity: Six or more symptoms of hyperactivity-impulsivity for children up to age 16 years, or five or more for adolescents age 17 years and older and adults; symptoms of hyperactivity-impulsivity have been present for at least 6 months to an extent that is disruptive and inappropriate for the person's developmental level:

- Often fidgets with or taps hands or feet, or squirms in seat.

- Often leaves seat in situations when remaining seated is expected.

- Often runs about or climbs in situations where it is not appropriate (adolescents or adults may be limited to feeling restless).

- Often unable to play or take part in leisure activities quietly.

- Is often "on the go" acting as if "driven by a motor".

- Often talks excessively.

- Often blurts out an answer before a question has been completed.

- Often has trouble waiting their turn.

- Often interrupts or intrudes on others (e.g., butts into conversations or games).

In addition, the following conditions must be met:

- Several inattentive or hyperactive-impulsive symptoms were present before age 12 years.

- Several symptoms are present in two or more settings, (such as at home, school, or work; with friends or relatives; or in other activities).

- There is clear evidence that the symptoms interfere with, or reduce the quality of, social, school, or work functioning.

- The symptoms are not better explained by another mental disorder (such as a mood disorder, anxiety disorder, dissociative disorder, or a personality disorder). The symptoms do not happen only during the course of schizophrenia or another psychotic disorder.

Combined hyperactive-impulsive and inattentive

- Six or more symptoms of inattention and six or more symptoms of hyperactivity-impulsivity are present.

- Most children have the combined type of ADHD.

What causes Attention- Deficit/ Hyperactivity Disorder (ADHD)

The exact causes of ADHD are still not completely understood. Many studies suggest that genes play a significant role in its development. ADHD most likely results from a combination of factors. In addition to genetics, researchers are exploring environmental factors, such as brain injuries, nutrition, and the social environment, which may contribute to ADHD.

Genes

Studies on twins worldwide have shown that ADHD often runs in families. Researchers examine several genes that may make people more likely to develop the disorder. Understanding these genes could potentially help prevent the condition before symptoms appear and lead to improved treatments.

Sugar

While some believe refined sugar can cause or worsen ADHD symptoms, more research contradicts this idea than supports it. Studies have tested sugar's effects on children's behavior and learning abilities, and the results have generally shown no significant differences between sugar and sugar substitutes.

However, in one study, children considered sugar-sensitive were given a sugar substitute called aspartame, also known as Nutrasweet. Surprisingly, when their mothers were told that their children had received sugar, they rated them as more hyperactive and critical compared to mothers who were told their children received aspartame.

Who is at risk of ADHD?

ADHD is one of the most common childhood disorders which can continue into adolescence and adulthood. It often starts around the age of seven. It affects approximately 4.1% of American adults aged 18 and older and 9.0% of American children aged 13 to 18. Boys are more commonly affected than girls. While the number of children diagnosed with ADHD is increasing, the reasons for this increase are unclear.

Diagnosis

Diagnosing ADHD can be challenging because children develop at different rates and have diverse personalities, temperaments, and energy levels. Symptoms usually appear early in life, often between the ages of three and six. They can vary significantly from person to person, making diagnosing difficult. Parents may notice their child losing interest in things sooner than others or constantly seeming "out of control." Teachers often observe symptoms when a child struggles to follow the rules or frequently daydreams in class or on the playground.

No single test can diagnose ADHD. Instead, a licensed health professional gathers information about the child's behavior in their environment. A pediatrician may assess or refer the child to a mental health specialist experienced in childhood mental health disorders like ADHD. Various factors, including medical conditions, learning disabilities, anxiety, depression, and external changes, can mimic ADHD-like symptoms.

Specialists may review school and medical records, consult with individuals close to the child, and assess behaviors in different settings to make an accurate diagnosis. They consider whether the behaviors are excessive, long-term, or a response to temporary situations. The child's behavior in various social situations, intellectual ability, and academic achievement are also evaluated.

- **Learning Disability:** In preschool, children with ADHD may struggle to understand certain sounds or words or work to express themselves verbally. School-aged children with ADHD might face reading, spelling, writing, and math difficulties.

- **Oppositional Defiant Disorder:** Children with this condition often display excessive stubbornness and rebellious behavior. They frequently engage in arguments with adults and refuse to follow the rules.

- **Conduct Disorder:** This condition involves a range of behaviors, such as lying, stealing, fighting, bullying, property destruction, breaking into homes, or using weapons. Children or teenagers with conduct disorder are also at a higher risk of using illegal substances and may face school or legal issues.

- **Anxiety and Depression:** Treating ADHD can sometimes help alleviate anxiety symptoms and certain forms of depression.

- **Bipolar Disorder:** Some children with ADHD may experience extreme mood swings, transitioning from mania (a significantly elevated mood) to depression quickly.

- **Tourette Syndrome:** While this brain disorder is rare in children, many who have it also have ADHD. Individuals with Tourette syndrome exhibit nervous tics and repetitive mannerisms, such as eye blinks, facial twitches, or grimacing. They may also clear their throats frequently, snort or sniff, or utter words inappropriately. Medications can be used to manage these behaviors.

ADHD may also co-occur with other conditions like sleep disorders, bed-wetting, substance use, and various illnesses. Detecting ADHD symptoms and seeking help early can lead to better outcomes for affected children and their families.

How is ADHD diagnosed in adults?

Many adults who have struggled with low performance in school and a series of low-paying jobs often wonder if they might have ADHD. Like children, adults who suspect they have ADHD should seek evaluation from a licensed mental health professional. Assessing adults for ADHD is more complex as their symptoms are often more varied and less straightforward than those in children.

To diagnose ADHD in adults, the individual must exhibit

symptoms that originated in childhood and persisted into adulthood. Health professionals utilize rating scales to assess if an adult meets the diagnostic criteria for ADHD. The professional also delves into the adult's childhood behavioral history and past school experiences. They interview spouses or partners, parents, close friends, and other associates. A physical examination and psychological tests are also part of the evaluation process.

For some adults, an ADHD diagnosis can provide a sense of relief. Those who have lived with the disorder since childhood but were not diagnosed may have developed negative self-perceptions over the many years. An ADHD diagnosis allows them to understand the root of their difficulties, and treatment can help them effectively manage ADHD.

CHAPTER 20
Treatments for ADHD

C urrently, available treatments focus on reducing the symptoms of ADHD and improving functioning. Treatments include medication, various types of psychotherapy, education, training, or a combination of treatments.

Treatments can relieve many of the disorder's symptoms, but there is no known cure. With treatment, most people with ADHD can be successful in school, their careers and go on to live and lead productive lives. Researchers are developing more effective treatments and interventions and using new tools, such as brain imaging, to understand ADHD better and to find more effective ways to treat and prevent it.

Medications

The most common medication used for treating ADHD is a 'stimulant.' A stimulant is a fast-acting prescribed medication that can make a person feel more aware, alert, attentive, and energetic. When used by children, it has a calming effect on them. There are different types of stimulant medications. There are other non-stimulant medications that work differently from a stimulant. In many children, ADHD medication reduces hyperactivity, and impulsivity and improves their ability to focus, work, and learn more effectively. The medication sometimes improves physical coordination.

A one-size-fits-all approach does not apply to all children with ADHD. What works for one child might not for another. One child might have side effects with a certain medication, while another may not. Sometimes doctors will try several medications or dosages before finding one that works for a particular child. Caregivers and doctors will closely and carefully monitor any child taking medication.

Stimulant medications come in different forms, such as pills, capsules, liquids, or skin patches. Some medications also come in short-acting, long-acting, or extended-release varieties. The active ingredient in each is the same, but it is released differently in the body. Long-acting or extended-release forms often allow a child to take it once a day before school. This prevents them from making a daily trip to the school nurse for another dosage. Parents and doctors should decide which medication is best for the child and whether the child needs medication only during school hours or during evenings and weekends.

Side effects of stimulant medications

Presently, available treatments primarily aim at alleviating the symptoms of ADHD and enhancing overall functioning. These treatments encompass medication, different forms of psychotherapy, educational interventions, training programs, or a combination of these approaches.

These treatments can effectively alleviate many of the disorder's symptoms. However, it's essential to note that there is currently no known cure for ADHD. Nevertheless, with proper treatment, most individuals with ADHD can excel in their academic pursuits and careers and lead productive lives.

Researchers continue to advance in developing more effective treatments and interventions for ADHD. They utilize innovative tools, such as brain imaging, to gain a better understanding of ADHD and to discover improved methods for treatment and prevention.

The most commonly reported side effects associated with stimulant medications are:

Decreased Appetite: Some individuals experience a decrease in appetite. If this side effect persists, it is essential to consult the child's doctor. Concerns about the child's growth or weight gain while on this medication should also be discussed with the doctor.

Sleep Problems: In some cases, individuals may have difficulty falling asleep. To address this issue, the doctor may recommend a lower dosage or a shorter-acting form of the medication. Adjusting the timing of medication administration, especially in the afternoon or evening, may be suggested. Establishing a consistent sleep routine with relaxing elements including warm milk, soft music, or quiet activities in dim light can help resolve sleep difficulties.

Less Common Side Effects: Some children may suddenly experience repetitive movements or tics. Altering the medication dosage might alleviate the tics. A personality change may also occur, such as appearing 'flat' or emotionless. Parents or caregivers should consult their child's primary care physician in such cases.

Are Stimulant Medications Safe?

Under medical supervision, stimulant medications are considered safe. These medications do not induce a 'high' in children with ADHD. While some children may report feeling slightly different or 'funny,' there is limited evidence to support concerns that stimulant medications may lead to substance abuse or dependence.

Do Medications Cure ADHD?

Currently, available medications do not offer a cure for ADHD. Instead, they help manage the symptoms as long as they are taken. Medications can improve a child's ability to focus, pay attention, and complete schoolwork. However, their impact on helping children learn or enhance their academic skills remains to be determined. Combining behavioral therapy, counseling, and practical support can further aid children with ADHD and their families better manage everyday challenges. Research funded by the National Institute of Mental Health (NIMH) has revealed that medication works most effectively when the prescribing doctor closely monitors the treatment and adjusts the dosage based on the child's needs.

Counseling/Psychotherapy

Various forms of psychotherapy are used to treat ADHD.

Behavioral therapy is focused on helping children modify their behavior. This may involve practical assistance, such as task organization and addressing emotionally challenging situations. Behavioral therapy also teaches children self-monitoring and how to provide self-praise or rewards for desired behavior.

Techniques for anger management and thinking before acting are valuable components of behavioral therapy. Parents and teachers can assist by offering feedback on various behaviors. Structured routines, including clear rules and chore lists, may also be beneficial in helping children manage their behavior.

Some social skill training programs aim to teach children how to interpret facial expressions, vocal tones in others, and appropriate responses to social cues.

How Can Parents Help?

Children with ADHD require guidance and understanding from their parents and teachers to reach their full potential in school and life. Before diagnosis, frustration, blame, and anger may have been evident within a family. Parents and children may need assistance in overcoming these negative emotions. Mental health professionals can provide education to parents about ADHD's impact on families and help both children and parents develop new skills, attitudes, and better ways of interacting.

Parenting skills training helps parents learn to use a system of rewards and consequences to modify a child's behavior. Parents are taught to provide immediate and positive feedback for behaviors they wish to encourage while ignoring or redirecting behaviors they want to discourage. Sometimes, parents may use 'time-outs' when a child's behavior becomes unmanageable. During a time-out, the child is briefly separated from the upsetting situation to calm down.

Parenting skill training also encourages parents to engage in enjoyable or relaxing activities with their children. Parents should acknowledge and highlight the child's strengths and abilities. Structuring situations more positively can also be beneficial, such as limiting the number of playmates to prevent overstimulation. Additionally, parents may benefit from learning stress management techniques that will enhance their ability to cope with frustration and respond calmly to their child's behavior.

In some cases, family therapy may be necessary, with therapists assisting family members in finding better strategies for handling disruptive behaviors and promoting behavioral changes. Support groups can also benefit parents and families, providing a platform to connect with others facing similar challenges and share experiences, recommended specialists, and strategies.

How is ADHD Treated in Adults?

Like children with ADHD, adults receive treatment through medication, psychotherapy, or a combination of these three approaches.

Medications

Prescribing stimulants and other medications for adults with ADHD involves careful consideration. Adults often take other medications for physical issues including diabetes, high blood pressure, or anxiety and depression. Some of these medications may interact poorly with stimulants. Therefore, adults with ADHD should consult with their doctors to explore suitable medication options. The doctor and patient must consider these and other factors when prescribing medication.

Education and Psychotherapy

Professional counselors or therapists can help adults with ADHD learn to better organize their lives through tools like calendars, date books, and reminder notes. Identifying a designated place for keys, bills, and paperwork can improve organization. Dividing large tasks into smaller, manageable steps offers a sense of accomplishment.

Psychotherapy, including cognitive-behavioral therapy, aims to enhance self-image by exploring the experiences that contributed to it. Therapists also encourage adults with ADHD to adapt to life changes associated with treatment, such as thinking before acting or avoiding unnecessary risks. (NIMH).

CHAPTER 21
Depression

Depression is a severe mental health condition beyond the typical moments of feeling blue or sad. While occasional bouts of sadness are fleeting and resolve within a few hours or days, depression significantly disrupts daily life and brings distress to those affected. This common yet severe illness requires attention. Regrettably, many individuals with depressive conditions choose not to seek treatment. However, most, including those grappling with severe depression, can significantly improve with appropriate interventions. Treatments such as medications, psychotherapy, and other methods effectively address depression.

Types of Depressive Disorders

Several forms of depressive disorders exist, each presenting distinct characteristics:

Major Depression: This form entails severe symptoms that interfere with a person's ability to function in various aspects of life, including work, sleep, study, and daily activities. While a major depressive episode can be a one-time occurrence, it often recurs, necessitating treatment.

Persistent Depressive Disorder: This disorder involves a prolonged, two-year period of persistent depressed mood.

Individuals diagnosed with this condition may experience

episodes of major depression interchanged with periods of less severe symptoms, but the overall duration must be two years.

Additionally, there are other types of depression with unique features, including:

Psychotic Depression: This condition combines severe depression with psychosis, characterized by delusions, hallucinations, or other false beliefs.

Postpartum Depression: Unlike the typical 'baby blues' experienced after childbirth, postpartum depression is a more severe and overwhelming condition. It affects an estimated 10 to 15 percent of women after giving birth.

Seasonal Affective Disorder (SAD): SAD occurs in winter when reduced sunlight leads to depression. While light therapy can be effective, many SAD sufferers do not respond to this treatment alone and may benefit from antidepressant medication or psychotherapy.

Bipolar Disorder: This condition, known as manic-depressive illness, involves mood swings cycling between extremes of mania (elevated mood) and depression.

What are the signs and symptoms of depression?

People with depressive illnesses do not all experience or display the same symptoms. The severity, frequency, and duration of symptoms vary depending on the individual and his or her particular mental illness.

Signs and symptoms include:

- Persistent sad, anxious, or 'empty' feelings.

- Feelings of hopelessness or pessimism.

- Feelings of guilt, worthlessness, or helplessness.

- Irritability, restlessness.

- Loss of interest in pleasurable activities such as sex, going on adventures, enjoying movies, or watching favorite shows or hobbies such as football, basketball, playing games, etc.

- Fatigue and decreased energy.

- Difficulty concentrating, remembering details, and making decisions.

- Insomnia, early-morning wakefulness, or excessive sleeping.

- Overeating or appetite loss.

- Thoughts of suicide, or suicide attempts.

- Aches or pains, headaches, cramps, or digestive problems that do not ease even with treatment.

CHAPTER 22
Obsessive-Compulsive Disorder (OCD)

Double-checking things is something many people do regularly, such as making sure they turn off the stove or iron before leaving home. However, for those with OCD, the need to repeatedly check things, experience specific thoughts, and perform repetitive routines or rituals becomes a distressing and disruptive part of daily life.

Obsessions: These are the frequent, upsetting thoughts that individuals with OCD encounter. They create a compelling urge to engage in particular rituals or behaviors known as compulsions in an attempt to control these thoughts. Individuals with OCD find it challenging to manage these obsessions and compulsions. OCD often emerges during childhood or adolescence, and individuals are typically diagnosed by the age of 19. Symptoms can fluctuate over time, with periods of exacerbation and improvement.

Causes of OCD: While OCD can have a familial component, the exact reasons why some people develop OCD remain unknown. Researchers have identified various brain regions involved in obsessive thoughts, compulsive behaviors, and associated fears and anxieties. This ongoing research aims to enhance treatment approaches. Stress and environmental factors are also areas of interest in understanding OCD.

Signs and Symptoms of OCD: People with OCD typically exhibit the following characteristics:

Obsessions: Repeated thoughts or images related to various themes, including fear of germs, dirt, intruders, acts of violence, harm to loved ones, sexual acts, conflicts with religious beliefs, or excessive tidiness.

Compulsions: Repeated rituals or behaviors like hand-washing, door-locking and unlocking, counting, hoarding unneeded items, or repeating specific actions.

Lack of Control: Inability to manage unwanted thoughts and behaviors.

Lack of Pleasure: Performing these behaviors doesn't bring pleasure but offers brief relief from the anxiety caused by the thoughts.

Time-Consuming: Spending at least one hour daily on these thoughts and rituals, causing distress and interfering with daily life.

Diagnosis and Treatment of OCD: To address OCD, begin by discussing your symptoms with your doctor, who will perform a physical examination to rule out underlying physical conditions. In many cases, your doctor may refer you to a mental health specialist.

OCD is generally treated through a combination of psychotherapy, medication, or both:

Psychotherapy: Cognitive behavioral therapy (CBT),

specifically Exposure and Response Prevention Therapy (ERP), is an effective method for managing OCD. These therapies teach individuals alternative ways of thinking, behaving, and reacting to situations, helping them better handle obsessive thoughts, reduce compulsive behaviors, and alleviate anxiety. ERP specifically targets intrusive thoughts and associated behaviors in individuals with OCD.

Medication

The use of medication can help in the treatment of OCD. The most commonly prescribed medications for OCD are antidepressants. Doctors use antidepressants to treat depression, but they are also particularly helpful for OCD. They may take several weeks (10 to 12 weeks) to start working. Some medications may cause side effects such as headache, nausea, or difficulty sleeping. When the medication dose starts low and is increased over time, the side effects are not usually severe. This is something that you will have to talk to your doctor about.

Combination of CBT and medication

There are those with OCD who do better with Cognitive and Behavioral Therapy (CBT), especially Exposure and Response Prevention Therapy. Others do better with medication, while some do best with a combination of the two. Many studies have shown that combining CBT with medication is the best approach for treating OCD, particularly in children and adolescents. It is very important that one's doctor is consulted in order to receive the best treatment recommendations.

CHAPTER 23

Paranoid Personality Disorder (PPD)

Paranoid Personality Disorder is classified within 'Cluster A' personality disorders, characterized by peculiar or eccentric thought patterns. It typically emerges during early adulthood and appears more prevalent among men than women.

Symptoms of PPD: Individuals with PPD often exhibit self-protective behavior, constantly vigilant and convinced that others are attempting to demean, harm, or threaten them. These unfounded beliefs hinder their ability to form close relationships. Common characteristics of those with PPD include:

- **Doubts About Others:** Questioning the commitment, loyalty, or trustworthiness of others, believing they are being used or deceived.

- **Reluctance to Share:** Hesitating to confide in others or reveal personal information due to the fear it will be exploited.

- **Unforgiving Nature:** Holding grudges and displaying hypersensitivity, particularly in response to criticism.

- **Interpretation of Hidden Meanings:** Perceiving hidden meanings in innocent remarks or casual glances by others.

- **Belief in Attacks on Character:** Sensing attacks on their character that go unnoticed by others and responding with anger and retaliation.

- **Unfounded Suspicions:** Develop recurrent, groundless suspicions, particularly regarding the fidelity of their partners, spouses, or lovers.

- **Difficulty in Relationships:** Maintaining cold and distant relationships, often exhibiting controlling and **jealous behaviors.**

- **Lack of Self-Awareness:** Failing to recognize their role in conflicts or problems, believing they are always right.

- **Inability to Relax:** Struggling to relax and frequently exhibiting hostility, stubbornness, and argumentative behavior.

Causes of PPD: The exact cause of PPD is not precisely known, but it likely results from a blend of biological and psychological factors. The increased occurrence of PPD in individuals with close relatives affected by schizophrenia implies a genetic link between these disorders. Early childhood experiences, including physical or emotional trauma, are also believed to contribute to PPD development.

How is PPD Diagnosed? When physical symptoms are present, the diagnostic process begins with a detailed medical and psychiatric history assessment and a physical examination when necessary. While there are no specific laboratory tests for diagnosing personality disorders, doctors use various diagnostic methods to rule out physical illness.

If no physical cause is identified, the individual may be referred to a psychiatrist or psychologist, specialists trained in diagnosing and treating mental illnesses. These professionals employ tailored interview and assessment tools to evaluate individuals for personality disorders.

Source: WebMD.

The next three chapters are case studies taken from the media.

CHAPTER 24
Protecting Your Heart

This article first appeared in October 2010 by Vidya Sury and then in another article in April 2015 written by Katherine Kam for WebMD.

Frequent anger and its association with heart disease should give 'ragers,' 'yellers,' and door slammers reason to pause. The consequences of letting anger run unchecked have taken on a new level of urgency, as recent findings reveal that recurrent high levels of anger may significantly elevate the risk of heart disease. Thus, the choice to vent frustrations through yelling or venting fury when confronted with stressful situations becomes a matter of potential life or death.

Addressing this concerning link between anger and heart disease, Laura Kubzansky, Ph.D., MPH, an associate professor at the Harvard School of Public Health in Cambridge, Mass., who specializes in the study of stress and emotions in cardiovascular disease, highlights the particular concern surrounding individuals who frequently experience intense anger. The emphasis here is on the frequency of such high levels of anger.

It is noteworthy that moderate anger may not be the culprit. Expressing anger healthily and reasonably can be beneficial. According to Kubzansky, the ability to express anger constructively is a functional and necessary aspect of human interaction. However, those who resort to explosive anger, involving object hurling or screaming, may find themselves at a greater risk of developing heart disease. Individuals who harbor suppressed or concealed anger also raise concern, as they may be vulnerable to similar cardiovascular risks. It is essential to understand that residing at either end of the anger spectrum holds its problems.

The precise mechanisms through which anger contributes to heart disease are not fully understood. However, compelling theories suggest that anger may induce direct physiological effects on the heart and arteries. Emotions like anger and hostility trigger a swift activation of the "fight or flight response," characterized by the release of stress hormones such as adrenaline and cortisol. These hormones cause an acceleration of heart rate and respiration, providing a sudden burst of energy. Simultaneously, blood pressure surges due to the constriction of blood vessels, contributing to the intricate relationship between anger and heart disease.

The physiological effects of anger on the heart

So how exactly does anger contribute to heart disease? Scientists don't know for sure, but anger might produce direct physiological effects on the heart and arteries. Emotions such as anger and hostility quickly activate the "fight or flight response," in which stress hormones, including adrenaline and cortisol, speed up your heart rate and breathing and give you a burst of energy. Blood pressure also rises as your blood vessels constrict.

While this stress response mobilizes you for emergencies, it might cause harm if activated repeatedly. "You get high cortisol and high adrenaline levels and that is the cardiotoxic effect of anger expression," says Jerry Kiffer, MA, a heart-brain researcher at the Cleveland Clinic's Psychological Testing Center. "It causes wear and tear on the heart and cardiovascular system." Frequent anger may speed up the process of atherosclerosis, in which fatty plaques build up in arteries, Kiffer says. The heart pumps harder, blood vessels constrict, blood pressure surges and there are higher levels of glucose in the blood and more fat globules in the blood vessels. All this, scientists believe, can cause damage to artery walls. Anger might not be the only culprit. In Kubzansky's research, she found that high levels of anxiety and depression may contribute to heart disease risk, too, "they tend to cooccur," she says. "People who are angry a lot tend to have other chronic negative emotions as well".

CHAPTER 25
Rick Warren's Story

This article first appeared on April 13, 2009, in an excerpt from "Prophet of Purpose" book written by Jeffrey Sheler interviewed by Christianity Today editor-in-chief David Neff.

The Rick Warren story: In an unauthorized biography shedding light on the life of "America's pastor," we gain insights into the unconventional origins of Rick Warren's marriage and the trials that fueled his transformation. Jeffery L. Sheler, U.S. News and World Report's religion correspondent, takes us on this journey within his latest work, "Prophet of Purpose: The Life of Rick Warren." The book unveils a more vulnerable side of the amiable yet self-assured megachurch pastor, who counts presidents and billionaires among his friends.

During a live web discussion with David Neff, editor-in-chief of Christianity Today, Sheler delved into the contents of the book and shared his reflections on the man he diligently interviewed and researched for months.

An intriguing aspect of Warren's biography lies in exploring his marriage. Despite appearances and the affirmations of those who know the couple well, Rick and Kay Warren's union had a far from auspicious beginning.

As Sheler recounts, on their wedding day, they were "virtual strangers." Hardships and misunderstandings marred their honeymoon, and profound marital problems plagued the early days of their marriage. The stress from these issues and Rick's demanding workload eventually landed him in the hospital. Meanwhile, Kay firmly held her conviction against divorce and felt she was committed to a life of suffering.

Faced with these challenges, the couple decided to seek marriage counseling, even though their financial situation at the time did not readily permit it. Rick resorted to putting

$1,500 on his credit card for the therapy, humorously quipping that "MasterCard saved my marriage!" This candid display of honesty, humility, and transparency underscores their remarkable journey. Today, they enjoy a flourishing and affectionate marriage. Their openness extends to the admission that they occasionally seek Christian marriage counseling to fine-tune their relationship.

Ed Stetzer, a prominent pastor and writer who advises evangelical churches, attests to their unwavering belief in the transformative power of God. He acknowledges that, while they firmly hold the conviction that Christ can mend all, there are moments when external assistance, both medical and psychological is indispensable in this process.

In a touching note, during the grief following the loss of Rick Warren's son, Rebekah Lyons, a blogger and the wife of the renowned pastor Gabe Lyons, candidly expressed her ongoing battle with anxiety and panic. She urged fellow Christians not to equate mental illness with spiritual weakness, highlighting the need for compassion, support, and understanding within faith communities.

This revelation has ignited conversations within church congregations, raising concerns about whether the strong emphasis on evangelical faith, prayer, and reliance on God and Jesus for healing could deter individuals from discussing mental illness or reaching out for assistance for themselves or their loved ones.

The Post's Sally Quinn talks with Saddleback Church co-founder Kay Warren on doubting God's existence, the HIV/Aids epidemic, and why God allows suffering. (From the archives: August 7, 2012) (The Washington Post)

"As Christians, we believe this side of heaven all disease, sickness, and pain are rooted in a world broken by sin. But there are real consequences to living amidst the mess. To oversimplify these complexities would be naive at best, negligent at worst," she wrote.

The revelation has spurred discussion within church communities about how a fervent belief among evangelicals in the power of prayer and dependence on God and Jesus for healing might stifle congregants from talking about mental illness or seeking help for themselves or family members.

For Christians who believe in turning to a divine source for emotional help, even defining a prayerful request can be fraught, some leaders and congregants pointed out. For example, is depression the result of sinful behavior for which one should seek forgiveness? And if prayer does not bring relief, what might God be saying?

When people suffer despite prayer and consider therapy, "people think: 'Is this a knock against my faith? Am I not believing in God enough? Now I have to resort to this?'" Said Henry Davis, leader of the evangelical First Baptist Church of Highland Park. "I believe God is in therapy. I believe God can be in medicine. If someone says, 'I'm just going to pray,' you have to do more."

Mike Fewster, a pastor at Chantilly's New Life Christian Church, can relate to Matthew Warren's struggles. Fewster, 44, fought various addictions and considered killing himself before he was hospitalized and diagnosed with bipolar disease. His problems led him to find a weekly support group to encourage others to open up, but about half of the group's members come from churches where they don't feel comfortable sharing their struggles.

"For a lot of people, the church is just a place they go, a building, they put on their suit and tie, stand up when they're told to and check a box, but that's not supposed to be church," he said. "There is this false idea that church people are perfect. I try to say: 'Until you break that, you'll never get healing.'"

CHAPTER 26
Creflo Dollar's Story

This article first appeared on June 8, 2012, on Charisma News.

According to Atlanta news reports from January 25, prosecutors have decided to dismiss the simple battery charge against a megachurch pastor in Atlanta, Georgia. This pastor, who had been accused of choking and hitting his teenage daughter, completed an anger management program. Initially, he faced charges of simple battery, family violence, and cruelty to children.

However, these charges were dropped after he successfully finished the anger management program. As reported by David Beasley of HuffPost on March 10, 2013, Creflo Dollar, the founder of World Changers Church International, a Christian congregation with nearly 30,000 members, underwent this program and covered approximately $1,000 in court fees as part of a pretrial intervention initiative, revealed Fayette County Solicitor General James Inagawa.

More often than not due to the stigma of Christians seeking counseling, they would rather go to their pastors which in turn can create mental health stress for the pastors, especially in the Black and Hispanic churches in the US. According to LifeWay Research dated August 2022, over half of pastors come in contact with parishioners with mental illnesses on a regular basis and about 26% of pastors have personally struggled with mental illness which proportionately is 23% of the general population. There are some things that pastors can do to help promote the health and well-being of their members. This includes establishing a counseling support ministry in collaboration with a local mental health agency and having open discussions and sermons addressing mental health issues.

Pastors can be effective advocates for mental health services by seeking such services for themselves to address many issues including burn-outs, stress, and moral failures. Pastors will be setting a great example for members who see counseling as stigmatizing and therefore should be avoided. I know many Christians who are not ashamed to admit their struggles with physical and medical illnesses. In like manner, they should not be ashamed to admit or acknowledge their mental health struggles and to seek appropriate treatment. If more Christians would engage in professional Christian counseling, I strongly believe that the church would be healthier and whole i.e., spiritually, mentally, emotionally, relationally, and physically. A survey done by the Presbyterian Church (USA) found that 44% of the 4,507 pastors surveyed reported that they" have not been trained to recognize mental illness or how to minister to those individuals and families who face them".

Many Christians, including prominent ones, have experienced stunning moral failures that have negatively impacted their functioning, marriages, families, and churches. Had they sought professional Christian counseling, many Christians would have avoided those pitfalls.

The truth is that none of us, irrespective of societal, religious, or economic status are immune to unethical behaviors that can be very costly if not addressed on time or appropriately. We all have issues, weaknesses, struggles, and wounds that sometimes require professional help, counseling, or support before they begin to impact our personal, relational, and spiritual relationships negatively. It is possible to be saved yet struggling, well, but wounded due to past or current indiscretions or issues.

There are approximately 350,000 religious organizations in the US, most having membership under 100. Most pastors do not have the training, tools, or resources to effectively help their congregants address some of the more serious mental and emotional issues that members have experienced or are presently experiencing. As a result, many Christians live their lives with unresolved hurt, pain, and heartbreak. Many pastors would have experienced and may still be challenged by chronic unresolved issues. Today, many mental, emotional, and relational challenges that are observed or expressed within the church are described, labeled, or approached as spiritual issues, often leading to long-term dissatisfaction with one's spiritual life because of no lasting or ongoing positive changes.

According to LifeWay Research, 48% of Evangelical Christians believe that mental illness, including depression and anxiety, can be cured by reading the Bible and praying more. Was this taught in the church, or is it a way out of avoiding the stigma of seeking professional counseling?

I do not believe that the response will be the same for those experiencing physical illnesses. This leads me to wonder how many marriages could have been saved, families and personal relationships could have been restored, careers and job promotions could have been attained, and illnesses could have been avoided if professional Christian counseling had been sought during those challenging situations. For many of you reading this book, today may not be too late.

Here is a list of reliable, Bible-based counseling organizations: www.aacc.net

www.biblicalcounseling.com www.christiancounseling.com www.focusonthefamily.com

www.psychologytoday.com-- On this website, you will have to explore the religious affiliation of the Christian counselor to make sure their doctrine is in alignment with yours.

www.totaltherapytoday.com

If this book has been a blessing to you, please leave a review on Amazon.com so that others can experience the same. Thank you!

1. Abe-Article Source: http://EzineArticles.com/2438125.

2. AllAboutCounseling.org.

3. David Powlison (2010). The Biblical Counseling Movement. New Growth Press, NC.

4. Eric L. Johnson (2010). Psychology and Christianity: Five views. IVP Academia: 2nd edition.

5. Focus on the Family.

6. https://www.thezebra.com/resources/research/mental-health-statistics/.

7. John Clark. The Benefits of Christian Counseling.

8. Karen B. Helmeke, Ph.D.; Catherine Ford Soni, Ph.D. (2004) The therapist notebook for integrating spirituality in counseling.

9. ManToManOnline.org.

10. National Campaign to prevent teen and unwanted pregnancy, 2001.

11. National Institute of Mental Health, Mental Health America, National Alliance on Mental Illness, Johns Hopkins Medicine, Centers for Disease Control, and Our World in Data.

12. Unless otherwise indicated, all scriptures are taken from the King James Bible version copyright 2016.

13. WebMD Magazine: Reviewed by Louise Chang, MD.

14. William T. Kirwan (1984). Biblical concepts in Christian counseling: A case for integrating psychology & theology. Baker Publishing Group, Grand Rapids, MI.

Please SCAN ME to leave a review on Amazon. Thanks

www.ingramcontent.com/pod-product-compliance
Lightning Source LLC
Chambersburg PA
CBHW051534120626
46551CB00012B/1212